ALFRED TENNYSON

BY

ANDREW LANG

SECOND EDITION

AMS PRESS
NEW YORK

Reprinted from the edition of 1901, Edinburgh
First AMS EDITION published 1970
Manufactured in the United States of America

Library of Congress Catalog Card Number: 70-111615
SBN: 404-03856-5

AMS PRESS, INC.
New York, N.Y. 10003

INTRODUCTION.

In writing this brief sketch of the Life of Tennyson, and this attempt to appreciate his work, I have rested almost entirely on the Biography by Lord Tennyson (with his kind permission) and on the text of the Poems. As to the Life, doubtless current anecdotes, not given in the Biography, are known to me, and to most people. But as they must also be familiar to the author of the Biography, I have not thought it desirable to include what he rejected. The works of the "localisers" I have not read: Tennyson disliked these researches, as a rule, and they appear to be unessential, and often hazardous. The professed commentators I have not consulted. It appeared better to give one's own impressions of the Poems, unaffected by the impressions of others, except in one or two cases where matters of fact rather than of taste seemed to be in question. Thus on two or three points I have ventured to differ from a distinguished living critic, and have given the reasons for my dissent. Professor Bradley's *Commentary on In Memoriam*[1] came out after this sketch was in print. Many of the comments cited by Mr Bradley from his predecessors appear to justify my neglect of these curious inquirers. The "difficulties" which they raise are not likely, as a rule, to present themselves to persons who read poetry "for human pleasure."

I have not often dwelt on parallels to be found in the works of earlier poets. In many cases Tennyson deliberately reproduced passages from Greek, Latin, and old Italian writers, just as Virgil did in the case of Homer, Theocritus, Apollonius Rhodius, and others. There are, doubtless, instances in which a phrase is unconsciously reproduced by automatic memory, from an English poet. But I am less inclined than Mr Bradley to think that unconscious reminiscence is more common in Tennyson than in the poets generally. I have not closely examined Keats and Shelley, for example, to see how far.

[1] Macmillan & Co.

CONTENTS.

TENNYSON.

I.

THE life and work of Tennyson present something like
the normal type of what, in circumstances as fortunate
as mortals may expect, the life and work of a modern
poet ought to be. A modern poet, one says, because
even poetry is now affected by the division of labour.
We do not look to the poet for a large share in the
practical activities of existence : we do not expect him,
like Æschylus and Sophocles, Theognis and Alcæus, to
take a conspicuous part in politics and war ; or even, as
in the Age of Anne, to shine among wits and in society.
Life has become, perhaps, too specialised for such
multifarious activities. Indeed, even in ancient days,
as a Celtic proverb and as the picture of life in the
Homeric epics prove, the poet was already a man
apart—not foremost among statesmen and rather backward among warriors. If we agree with a not un-

A

popular opinion, the poet ought to be a kind of
"Titanic" force, wrecking himself on his own passions
and on the nature of things, as did Byron, Burns,
Marlowe, and Musset. But Tennyson's career followed
lines really more normal, the lines of the life of Wordsworth, wisdom and self-control directing the course of a
long, sane, sound, and fortunate existence. The great
physical strength which is commonly the basis of great
mental vigour was not ruined in Tennyson by poverty
and passion, as in the case of Burns, nor in forced
literary labour, as in those of Scott and Dickens. For
long he was poor, like Wordsworth and Southey, but
never destitute. He made his early effort : he had his
time of great sorrow, and trial, and apparent failure.
With practical wisdom he conquered circumstances ; he
became eminent ; he outlived reaction against his
genius ; he died in the fulness of a happy age and of
renown. This full-orbed life, with not a few years of
sorrow and stress, is what Nature seems to intend for
the career of a divine minstrel. If Tennyson missed
the "one crowded hour of glorious life," he had not
to be content in "an age without a name."

It was not Tennyson's lot to illustrate any modern
theory of the origin of genius. Born in 1809 of a
Lincolnshire family, long connected with the soil but
inconspicuous in history, Tennyson had nothing Celtic
in his blood, as far as pedigrees prove. This is unfortunate for one school of theorists. His mother
(genius is presumed to be derived from mothers) had a

genius merely for moral excellence and for religion. She is described in the poem of *Isabel*, and was "a remarkable and saintly woman." In the male line, the family was not (as the families of genius ought to be) brief of life and unhealthy. "The Tennysons never die," said the sister who was betrothed to Arthur Hallam. The father, a clergyman, was, says his grandson, "a man of great ability," and his "excellent library" was an element in the education of his family. "My father was a poet," Tennyson said, "and could write regular verse very skilfully." In physical type the sons were tall, strong, and unusually dark : Tennyson, when abroad, was not taken for an Englishman ; at home, strangers thought him "foreign." Most of the children had the temperament, and several of the sons had some of the accomplishments, of genius : whence derived by way of heredity is a question beyond conjecture, for the father's accomplishment was not unusual. As Walton says of the poet and the angler, they "were born to be so" : we know no more.

The region in which the paternal hamlet of Somersby lies, "a land of quiet villages, large fields, grey hillsides, and noble tall-towered churches, on the lower slope of a Lincolnshire wold," does not appear to have been rich in romantic legend and tradition. The folk-lore of Lincolnshire, of which examples have been published, does indeed seem to have a peculiar poetry of its own, but it was rather the humorous than the poetical aspect of the country-people that Tennyson appears to have

known.   In brief, we have nothing to inform us as to
how genius came into that generation of Tennysons
which was born between 1807 and 1819.   A source and
a cause there must have been, but these things are
hidden, except from popular science.

Precocity is not a sign of genius, but genius is perhaps
always accompanied by precocity.   This is especially
notable in the cases of painting, music, and mathematics ; but in the matter of literature genius may chiefly
show itself in acquisition, as in Sir Walter Scott, who
when a boy knew much, but did little that would attract
notice.   As a child and a boy young Tennyson was
remarked both for acquisition and performance.   His
own reminiscences of his childhood varied somewhat in
detail.   In one place we learn that at the age of eight
he covered a slate with blank verse in the manner of
Jamie Thomson, the only poet with whom he was then
acquainted.   In another passage he says, "The first
poetry that moved me was my own at five years old.
When I was eight I remember making a line I thought
grander than Campbell, or Byron, or Scott.   I rolled it
out, it was this—

' With slaughterous sons of thunder rolled the flood '—

great nonsense, of course, but I thought it fine ! "

It *was* fine, and was thoroughly Tennysonian.   Scott,
Campbell, and Byron probably never produced a line
with the qualities of this nonsense verse.   " Before I
could read I was in the habit on a stormy day of spread-

ing my arms to the wind and crying out, 'I hear a voice that's speaking in the wind,' and the words 'far, far away' had always a strange charm for me." A late lyric has this overword, *Far, far away !*

A boy of eight who knew the contemporary poets was more or less precocious. Tennyson also knew Pope, and wrote hundreds of lines in Pope's measure. At twelve the boy produced an epic, in Scott's manner, of some six thousand lines. He "never felt himself more truly inspired," for the sense of "inspiration" (as the late Mr Myers has argued in an essay on the "Mechanism of Genius") has little to do with the actual value of the product. At fourteen Tennyson wrote a drama in blank verse. A chorus from this play (as one guesses), a piece from "an unpublished drama written very early," is published in the volume of 1830 :—

> "The varied earth, the moving heaven,
>   The rapid waste of roving sea,
> The fountain-pregnant mountains riven
>   To shapes of wildest anarchy,
> By secret fire and midnight storms
>   That wander round their windy cones."

These lines are already Tennysonian. There is the classical transcript, "the varied earth," *dædala tellus.* There is the geological interest in the forces that shape the hills. There is the use of the favourite word "windy," and later in the piece—

> "The troublous autumn's *sallow* gloom."

The young poet from boyhood was original in his manner.

Byron made him *blasé* at fourteen. Then Byron died, and Tennyson scratched on a rock "Byron is dead," on "a day when the whole world seemed darkened for me." Later he considered Byron's poetry "too much akin to rhetoric." "Byron is not an artist or a thinker, or a creator in the higher sense, but a strong personality; he is endlessly clever, and is now unduly depreciated." He "did give the world another heart and new pulses, and so we are kept going." But "he was dominated by Byron till he was seventeen, when he put him away altogether."

In his boyhood, despite the sufferings which he endured for a while at school at Louth; despite bullying from big boys and masters, Tennyson would "shout his verses to the skies." "Well, Arthur, I mean to be famous," he used to say to one of his brothers. He observed nature very closely by the brook and the thundering sea-shores: he was never a sportsman, and his angling was in the manner of the lover of *The Miller's Daughter*. He was seventeen (1826) when *Poems by Two Brothers* (himself and his brother Charles) was published with the date 1827. These poems contain, as far as I have been able to discover, nothing really Tennysonian. What he had done in his own manner was omitted, "being thought too much out of the common for the public taste." The young poet had already saving common-sense, and understood the public. Fragments of the true gold are found in the volume of 1830, others are preserved in the Biography. The ballad suggested by *The Bride of Lammermoor* was not unworthy of Beddoes, and that novel, one cannot but think, suggested the opening situation in *Maud*, where the hero is a modern Master of Ravenswood in his relation to the rich interloping family and the beautiful daughter. To this point we shall return. It does not appear that Tennyson was conscious in *Maud* of the suggestion from Scott, and the coincidence may be merely accidental.

The Lover's Tale, published in 1879, was mainly a work of the poet's nineteenth year. A few copies had been printed for friends. One of these, with errors of the press, and without the intended alterations, was pirated by an unhappy man in 1875. In old age Tennyson brought out the work of his boyhood. "It was written before I had ever seen Shelley, though it is called Shelleyan," he said; and indeed he believed that his work had never been imitative, after his earliest efforts in the manner of Thomson and of Scott. The only things in *The Lover's Tale* which would suggest that the poet here followed Shelley are the Italian scene of the story, the character of the versification, and the extraordinary luxuriance and exuberance of the imagery.[1] As early as

---

[1] To the present writer, as to others, *The Lover's Tale* appeared to be imitative of Shelley, but if Tennyson had never read Shelley, *cadit quæstio*.

1868 Tennyson heard that written copies of *The Lover's Tale* were in circulation. He then remarked, as to the exuberance of the piece : "Allowance must be made for abundance of youth. It is rich and full, but there are mistakes in it. . . . The poem is the breath of young love."

How truly Tennysonian the manner is may be understood even from the opening lines, full of the original cadences which were to become so familiar :—

> " Here far away, seen from the topmost cliff,
> Filling with purple gloom the vacancies
> Between the tufted hills, the sloping seas
> Hung in mid-heaven, and half way down rare sails,
> White as white clouds, floated from sky to sky."

The narrative in parts one and two (which alone were written in youth) is so choked with images and descriptions as to be almost obscure. It is the story, practically, of a love like that of Paul and Virginia, but the love is not returned by the girl, who prefers the friend of the narrator. Like the hero of *Maud*, the speaker has a period of madness and illusion ; while the third part, "The Golden Supper"—suggested by a story of Boccaccio, and written in maturity—is put in the mouth of another narrator, and is in a different style. The discarded lover, visiting the vault which contains the body of his lady, finds her alive, and restores her to her husband. The whole finished legend is necessarily not among the author's masterpieces. But perhaps not even Keats in his earliest work displayed more of

promise, and gave more assurance of genius. Here
and there come turns and phrases, "all the charm of
all the Muses," which remind a reader of things later
well known in pieces more mature. Such lines are—

> " Strange to me and sweet,
> Sweet through strange years,"

and—

> " Like to a low-hung and a fiery sky
>
> . . . .
>
> Hung round with *ragged rims* and burning folds."

And—

> " Like sounds without the twilight realm of dreams,
> Which wander round the bases of the hills."

We also note close observation of nature in the curious
phrase—

> " Cries of the partridge like a rusty key
> Turned in a lock."

Of this kind was Tennyson's adolescent vein, when
he left

> " The poplars four
> That stood beside his father's door,"

and the Somersby brook, and the mills and granges, the
seas of the Lincolnshire coast, and the hills and dales
among the wolds, for Cambridge. He was well read in
old and contemporary English literature, and in the
classics. Already he was acquainted with the singular
trance-like condition to which his poems occasionally
allude, a subject for comment later. He matriculated at

Trinity, with his brother Charles, on February 20, 1828, and had an interview of a not quite friendly sort with a proctor before he wore the gown.

That Tennyson should go to Cambridge, not to Oxford, was part of the nature of things, by which Cambridge educates the majority of English poets, whereas Oxford has only "turned out" a few—like Shelley.   At that time, as in Macaulay's day, the path of university honours at Cambridge lay through Mathematics, and, except for his prize poem in 1829, Tennyson took no honours at all.   His classical reading was pursued as literature, not as a course of grammar and philology.   No English poet, at least since Milton, had been better read in the classics ; but Tennyson's studies did not aim at the gaining of academic distinction.   His aspect was such that Thompson, later Master of Trinity, on first seeing him come into hall, said, " That man must be a poet."   Like Byron, Shelley, and probably Coleridge, Tennyson looked the poet that he was : " Six feet high, broad-chested, strong-limbed, his face Shakespearian and with deep eyelids, his forehead ample, crowned with dark wavy hair, his head finely poised."

Not much is recorded of Tennyson as an undergraduate.   In our days efforts would have been made to enlist so promising a recruit in one of the college boats ; but rowing was in its infancy.   It is a peculiarity of the universities that little flocks of men of unusual ability come up at intervals together, breaking the monotony of idlers, prize scholars, and honours men.

Such a group appeared at Balliol in Matthew Arnold's time, and rather later, at various colleges, in the dawn of Pre-Raphaelitism. The Tennysons—Alfred, Frederick, and Charles — were members of such a set. There was Arthur Hallam, son of the historian, from Eton ; there was Spedding, the editor and biographer of Bacon ; Milnes (Lord Houghton), Blakesley (Dean of Lincoln), Thompson, Merivale, Trench (a poet, and later, Archbishop of Dublin), Brookfield, Buller, and, after Tennyson the greatest, Thackeray, a contemporary if not an "Apostle." Charles Buller's, like Hallam's, was to be an "unfulfilled renown." Of Hallam, whose name is for ever linked with his own, Tennyson said that he would have been a great man, but not a great poet ; "he was as near perfection as mortal man could be." His scanty remains are chiefly notable for his divination of Tennyson as a great poet ; for the rest, we can only trust the author of *In Memoriam* and the verdict of tradition.

The studies of the poet at this time included original composition in Greek and Latin verse, history, and a theme that he alone has made poetical, natural science. All poetry has its roots in the age before natural science was more than a series of nature-myths. The poets have usually, like Keats, regretted the days when

" There was an awful rainbow once in heaven,"

when the hills and streams were not yet " dispeopled of their dreams." Tennyson, on the other hand, was already finding material for poetry in the world as seen through microscope and telescope, and as developed through " æonian " processes of evolution. In a note-book, mixed with Greek, is a poem on the Moon—not the moon of Selene, " the orbed Maiden," but of astronomical science. *In Memoriam* recalls the con-versations on labour and politics, discussions of the age of the Reform Bill, of rick-burning (expected to " make taters cheaper "), and of Catholic emancipation ; also the emancipation of such negroes as had not yet tasted the blessings of freedom. In politics Tennyson was what he remained, a patriot, a friend of freedom, a foe of disorder. His politics, he said, were those " of Shakespeare, Bacon, and every sane man." He was one of the Society of Apostles, and characteristically contributed an essay on Ghosts. Only the preface survives : it is not written in a scientific style ; but bids us " not assume that any vision *is* baseless." Perhaps the author went on to discuss " veridical hallucinations," but his ideas about these things must be considered later.

It was by his father's wish that Tennyson competed for the English prize poem. The theme, Timbuctoo, was not inspiring. Thackeray wrote a good parody of the ordinary prize poem in Pope's metre :—

" I see her sons the hill of glory mount,
    And sell their sugars on their own account ;
    Prone to her feet the prostrate nations come,
    Sue for her rice and barter for her rum."

Tennyson's work was not much more serious : he merely patched up an old piece, in blank verse, on the battle of Armageddon. The poem is not destitute of Tennysonian cadence, and ends, not inappropriately, with " All was night." Indeed, all *was* night.

An ingenious myth accounts for Tennyson's success : At Oxford, says Charles Wordsworth, the author was more likely to have been rusticated than rewarded. But already (1829) Arthur Hallam told Mr Gladstone that Tennyson "promised fair to be the greatest poet of our generation, perhaps of our century."

In 1830 Tennyson published the first volume of which he was sole author. Browning's *Pauline* was of the year 1833. It was the very dead hours of the Muses. The great Mr Murray had ceased, as one despairing of song, to publish poetry. Bulwer Lytton, in the preface to *Paul Clifford* (1830), announced that poetry, with every other form of literature except the Novel, was unremunerative and unread. Coleridge and Scott were silent : indeed Sir Walter was near his death ; Wordsworth had shot his bolt, though an arrow or two were left in the quiver. Keats, Shelley, and Byron were dead ; Milman's brief vogue was departing. It seemed as if novels alone could appeal to readers, so great a change in taste had been wrought by the sixteen years of Waverley romances. The slim volume of Tennyson was naturally neglected, though Leigh Hunt reviewed it in the *Tatler*. Hallam's comments in the *Englishman's Magazine*, though en-

thusiastic (as was right and natural), were judicious.
" The author imitates no one." Coleridge did not
read all the book, but noted "things of a good deal
of beauty. The misfortune is that he has begun to
write verses without very well understanding what
metre is." As Tennyson said in 1890, " So I, an
old man, who get a poem or poems every day, might
cast a casual glance at a book, and seeing something
which I could not scan or understand, might possibly
decide against the book without further consideration."
As a rule, the said books are worthless. The number
of versifiers makes it hard, indeed, for the poet to win
recognition. One little new book of rhyme is so like
another, and almost all are of so little interest!

The rare book that differs from the rest has a
bizarrerie with its originality, and in the poems of
1830 there was, assuredly, more than enough of the
bizarre. There were no hyphens in the double epithets,
and words like " tendriltwine" seemed provokingly
affected. A kind of lusciousness, like that of Keats
when under the influence of Leigh Hunt, may here
and there be observed. Such faults as these catch the
indifferent eye when a new book is first opened, and
the volume of 1830 was probably condemned by almost
every reader of the previous generation who deigned to
afford it a glance. Out of fifty-six pieces only twenty-
three were reprinted in the two volumes of 1842, which
won for Tennyson the general recognition of the world
of letters. Five or six of the pieces then left out were

added as *Juvenilia* in the collected works of 1871, 1872.
The whole mass deserves the attention of students of
the poet's development.

This early volume may be said to contain, in the
germ, all the great original qualities of Tennyson,
except the humour of his rural studies and the elaboration of his Idylls.   For example, in *Mariana* we
first note what may be called his perfection and
mature accomplishment.   The very few alterations
made later are verbal.   The moated grange of
Mariana in *Measure for Measure*, and her mood of
desertion and despair, are elaborated by a precision of
truth and with a perfection of harmony worthy of
Shakespeare himself, and minutely studied from the
natural scenes in which the poet was born.   If these
verses alone survived out of the wreck of Victorian
literature, they would demonstrate the greatness of the
author as clearly as do the fragments of Sappho.   *Isabel*
(a study of the poet's mother) is almost as remarkable
in its stately dignity ; while *Recollections of the Arabian
Nights* attest the power of refined luxury in romantic
description, and herald the unmatched beauty of *The
Lotos-Eaters*.   *The Poet*, again, is a picture of that
ideal which Tennyson himself was to fulfil ; and *Oriana*
is a revival of romance, and of the ballad, not limited to
the ballad form as in its prototype, *Helen of Kirkconnell*.
Curious and exquisite experiment in metre is indicated
in the *Leonine Elegiacs*, in *Claribel*, and several other
poems.   Qualities which were not for long to find public

expression, speculative powers brooding, in various moods, on ultimate and insoluble questions, were attested by *The Mystic*, and *Supposed Confessions of a Second-rate Sensitive Mind not in Unity with Itself*, an unlucky title of a remarkable performance. " In this, the most agitated of all his poems, we find the soul urging onward

> ' Thro' utter dark a full-sail'd skiff,
> Unpiloted i' the echoing dance
> Of reboant whirlwinds ; '

and to the question, ' Why not believe, then ? ' we have as answer a simile of the sea, which cannot slumber like a mountain tarn, or

> ' Draw down into his vexed pools
> All that blue heaven which hues and paves '

the tranquil inland mere." [1]

The poet longs for the faith of his infant days and of his mother—

> " Thy mild deep eyes upraised, that knew
> The beauty and repose of faith,
> And the clear spirit shining thro'."

That faith is already shaken, and the long struggle for belief has already begun.

Tennyson, according to Matthew Arnold, was not *un esprit puissant*. Other and younger critics, who have attained to a cock-certain mood of negation, are apt to blame him because, in fact, he did not finally agree with

---

[1] F. W. H. Myers, *Science and a Future Life*, p. 133.

their opinions. If a man is necessarily a weakling or a hypocrite because, after trying all things, he is not an atheist or a materialist, then the reproach of insincerity or of feebleness of mind must rest upon Tennyson. But it is manifest that, almost in boyhood, he had already faced the ideas which, to one of his character, almost meant despair : he had not kept his eyes closed. To his extremely self-satisfied accusers we might answer, in lines from this earliest volume (*The Mystic*) :—

> " Ye scorn him with an undiscerning scorn ;
> Ye cannot read the marvel in his eye,
> The still serene abstraction."

He would behold

> " One shadow in the midst of a great light,
> One reflex from eternity on time,
> One mighty countenance of perfect calm,
> Awful with most invariable eyes."

His mystic of these boyish years—

> " Often lying broad awake, and yet
> Remaining from the body, and apart
> In intellect and power and will, hath heard
> Time flowing in the middle of the night,
> And all things creeping to a day of doom."

In this poem, never republished by the author, is an attempt to express an experience which in later years he more than once endeavoured to set forth in articulate speech, an experience which was destined to colour his final speculations on ultimate problems of God and of the

B

soul. We shall later have to discuss the opinion of an eminent critic, Mr Frederic Harrison, that Tennyson's ideas, theological, evolutionary, and generally speculative, "followed, rather than created, the current ideas of his time." "The train of thought" (in *In Memoriam*), writes Mr Harrison, "is essentially that with which ordinary English readers had been made familiar by F. D. Maurice, Professor Jowett, Dr Martineau, *Ecce Homo*, *Hypatia*." Of these influences only Maurice, and Maurice only orally, could have reached the author of *The Mystic* and the *Supposed Confessions*. *Ecce Homo*, *Hypatia*, Mr Jowett, were all in the bosom of the future when *In Memoriam* was written. Now, *The Mystic* and the *Supposed Confessions* are prior to *In Memoriam*, earlier than 1830. Yet they already contain the chief speculative tendencies of *In Memoriam ;* the growing doubts caused by evolutionary ideas (then familiar to Tennyson, though not to "ordinary English readers"), the longing for a return to childlike faith, and the mystical experiences which helped Tennyson to recover a faith that abode with him. In these things he was original. Even as an undergraduate he was not following "a train of thought made familiar" by authors who had not yet written a line, and by books which had not yet been published.

So much, then, of the poet that was to be and of the philosopher existed in the little volume of the under-graduate. In *The Mystic* we notice a phrase, two words long, which was later to be made familiar, "Daughters

of time, divinely tall," reproduced in the picture of
Helen :—

> "A daughter of the Gods, divinely tall,
> And most divinely fair."

The reflective pieces are certainly of more interest now
(though they seem to have satisfied the poet less) than
the gallery of airy fairy Lilians, Adelines, Rosalinds, and
Eleänores :—

> "Daughters of dreams and of stories,"

like

> "Faustine, Fragoletta, Dolores,
> Félise, and Yolande, and Juliette."

Cambridge, which he was soon to leave, did not
satisfy the poet. Oxford did not satisfy Gibbon, or
later, Shelley; and young men of genius are not, in
fact, usually content with universities which, perhaps,
are doing their best, but are neither governed nor
populated by minds of the highest and most original
class.

> "You that do profess to teach
> And teach us nothing, feeding not the heart."

The universities, in fact, teach a good deal of that
which can be learned, but the best things cannot be
taught. The universities give men leisure, books, and
companionship, to learn for themselves. All tutors
cannot be, and at that time few dreamed of being,
men like Jowett and T. H. Green, Gamaliels at
whose feet undergraduates sat with enthusiasm, "did

eagerly frequent," like Omar Khayyám. In later years Tennyson found closer relations between dons and undergraduates, and recorded his affection for his university. She had supplied him with such companionship as is rare, and permitted him to "catch the blossom of the flying terms," even if tutors and lecturers were creatures of routine, *terriblement enfoncés dans la matière*, like the sire of Madelon and Cathos, that honourable citizen.

Tennyson just missed, by going down, a visit of Wordsworth to Cambridge. The old enthusiast of revolution was justifying passive obedience: thirty years had turned the almost Jacobin into an almost Jacobite. Such is the triumph of time. In the summer of 1830 Tennyson, with Hallam, visited the Pyrenees. The purpose was political—to aid some Spanish rebels. The fruit is seen in *Œnone* and *Mariana in the South*.

In March 1831 Tennyson lost his father. "He slept in the dead man's bed, earnestly desiring to see his ghost, but no ghost came." "You see," he said, "ghosts do not generally come to imaginative people;" a remark very true, though ghosts are attributed to "imagination." Whatever causes these phantasms, it is not the kind of *phantasia* which is consciously exercised by the poet. Coleridge had seen far too many ghosts to believe in them; and Coleridge and Donne apart, with the hallucinations of Goethe and Shelley, who met themselves, what poet ever did "see a ghost "? One who saw Tennyson as he wandered alone at this period called him "a mysterious being, seemingly lifted high above other mortals, and having a power of intercourse with the spirit world not granted to others." But it was the world of the poet, not of the "medium."

The Tennysons stayed on at the parsonage for six years. But, anticipating their removal, Arthur Hallam in 1831 dealt in prophecy about the identification in the district of places in his friend's poems — "critic after critic will trace the wanderings of the brook," as, in fact, critic after critic has done. Tennyson disliked these "localisers." The poet's walks were shared by Arthur Hallam, then affianced to his sister Emily.

II.

POEMS OF 1831-1833.

By 1832 most of the poems of Tennyson's second volume were circulating in MS. among his friends, and no poet ever had friends more encouraging. Perhaps bards of to-day do not find an eagerness among their acquaintance for effusions in manuscript, or in proof-sheets. The charmed volume appeared at the end of the year (dated 1833), and Hallam denounced as "infamous" Lockhart's review in the *Quarterly*. Infamous or not, it is extremely diverting. How Lockhart could miss the great and abundant poetry remains a marvel. Ten years later the Scorpion repented, and invited Sterling to review any book he pleased, for the purpose of enabling him to praise the two volumes of 1842, which he did gladly. Lockhart hated all affectation and "preciosity," of which the new book was not destitute. He had been among Words-worth's most ardent admirers when Wordsworth had few, but the memories of the war with the "Cockney School" clung to him, the war with Leigh Hunt, and now he gave himself up to satire. Probably he thought that the poet was a member of a London clique. There is really no excuse for Lockhart, except that he *did* repent, that much of his banter was amusing, and that, above all, his censures were accepted by the poet, who altered, later, many passages of a fine absurdity criticised by the infamous reviewer. One could name great prose-writers, historians, who never altered the wondrous errors to which their attention was called by critics. Prose-writers have been more sensitively attached to their glaring blunders in verifiable facts than was this very sensitive poet to his occasional lapses in taste.

The Lady of Shalott, even in its early form, was more than enough to give assurance of a poet. In effect it is even more poetical, in a mysterious way, if infinitely less human, than the later treatment of the same or a similar legend in *Elaine*. It has the charm of Coleridge, and an allegory of the fatal escape from the world of dreams and shadows into that of realities may have been really present to the mind of the young poet, aware that he was "living in phantasy." The alterations are usually for the better. The daffodil is not an aquatic plant, as the poet seems to assert in the first form—

> " The yellow-leavèd water-lily,
> The green sheathed daffodilly,
> Tremble in the water chilly,
> Round about Shalott."

Nobody can prefer to keep

> " Though the squally east wind keenly
> Blew, with folded arms serenely
> By the water stood the queenly
> Lady of Shalott."

However stoical the Lady may have been, the reader
is too seriously sympathetic with her inevitable discom-
fort—

> " All raimented in snowy white
> That loosely flew, "

as she was. The original conclusion was distressing;
we were dropped from the airs of mysterious
romance :—

> " They crossed themselves, their stars they blest,
> Knight, minstrel, abbot, squire, and guest ;
> There lay a parchment on her breast,
> That puzzled more than all the rest
> The well-fed wits at Camelot."

Hitherto we have been "puzzled," but as with the sublime incoherences of a dream. Now we meet well-fed
wits, who say, " Bless my stars ! " as perhaps we should
also have done in the circumstances—a dead lady arriving,
in a very cold east wind, alone in a boat, for " her blood
was frozen slowly," as was natural, granting the weather
and the lady's airy costume. It is certainly matter of
surprise that the young poet's vision broke up in this
humorous manner. And, after all, it is less surprising
that the Scorpion, finding such matter in a new little book

by a new young man, was more sensitive to the absurdity
than to the romance.   But no lover of poetry should
have been blind to the almost flawless excellence of
Mariana in the South, inspired by the landscape of the
Provençal tour with Arthur Hallam.   In consequence
of Lockhart's censures, or in deference to the maturer
taste of the poet, *The Miller's Daughter* was greatly
altered before 1842.   It is one of the earliest, if not
the very earliest, of Tennyson's domestic English idylls,
poems with conspicuous beauties, but not without
sacrifices to that Muse of the home affections on whom
Sir Barnes Newcome delivered his famous lecture.   The
seventh stanza perhaps hardly deserved to be altered, as
it is, so as to bring in "minnows" where "fish" had
been the reading, and where "trout" would best recall
an English chalk stream.   To the angler the rising
trout, which left the poet cold, is at least as welcome
as "the reflex of a beauteous form."   "Every woman
seems an angel at the water-side," said "that good old
angler, now with God," Thomas Tod Stoddart, and
so "the long and listless boy" found it to be.   It is no
wonder that the mother was "*slowly* brought to yield
consent to my desire."   The domestic affections, in
fact, do not adapt themselves so well to poetry as the
passion, unique in Tennyson, of *Fatima*.   The critics
who hunt for parallels or plagiarisms will note—

> "O Love, O fire! once he drew
> With one long kiss my whole soul thro'
> My lips,"

and will observe Mr Browning's

> " Once he kissed
> My soul out in a fiery mist."

As to *Œnone*, the scenery of that earliest of the
classical idylls is borrowed from the Pyrenees and the
tour with Hallam. "It is possible that the poem may
have been suggested by Beattie's *Judgment of Paris*,"
says Mr Collins ; it is also possible that the tale which

> " Quintus Calaber
> Somewhat lazily handled of old "

may have reached Tennyson's mind from an older
writer than Beattie. He is at least as likely to have
been familiar with Greek myth as with the lamented
"Minstrel."   The form of 1833, greatly altered in
1842, contained such unlucky phrases as "cedar
shadowy," and "snowycoloured," "marblecold," "violet-
eyed"—easy spoils of criticism.   The alterations which
converted a beautiful but faulty into a beautiful and
flawless poem perhaps obscure the significance of
Œnone's "I will not die alone," which in the earlier
volume directly refers to the foreseen end of all as
narrated in Tennyson's late piece, *The Death of
Œnone*. The whole poem brings to mind the glowing
hues of Titian and the famous Homeric lines on the
divine wedlock of Zeus and Hera.

The allegory or moral of *The Palace of Art* does not
need explanation. Not many of the poems owe more
to revision. The early stanza about Isaiah, with fierce

Ezekiel, and "Eastern Confutzee," did undeniably remind the reader, as Lockhart said, of *The Groves of Blarney*.

> "With statues gracing that noble place in,
> All haythen goddesses most rare,
> Petrarch, Plato, and Nebuchadnezzar,
> All standing naked in the open air."

In the early version the Soul, being too much "up to date,"

> "Lit white streams of dazzling gas,"

like Sir Walter Scott at Abbotsford.

> "Thus her intense, untold delight,
> In deep or vivid colour, smell, and sound,
> Was flattered day and night."

Lockhart was not fond of Sir Walter's experiments in gas, the "smell" gave him no "deep, untold delight," and his "infamous review" was biassed by these circumstances.

The volume of 1833 was in nothing more remarkable than in its proof of the many-sidedness of the author. He offered mediæval romance, and classical perfection touched with the romantic spirit, and domestic idyll, of which *The May Queen* is probably the most popular example. The "mysterious being," conversant with "the spiritual world," might have been expected to disdain topics well within the range of Eliza Cook. He did not despise but elevated them, and thereby did more to introduce himself to the wide English public than he could have done by a century of *Fatimas* or *Lotos-*

Eaters. On the other hand, a taste more fastidious, or more perverse, will scarcely be satisfied with pathos which in process of time has come to seem "obvious." The pathos of early death in the prime of beauty is less obvious in Homer, where Achilles is to be the victim, or in the laments of the Anthology, where we only know that the dead bride or maiden was fair ; but the poor May Queen is of her nature rather commonplace.

> "That good man, the clergyman, has told me words of
>   peace,"

strikes a note rather resembling the Tennysonian parody of Wordsworth—

> "A Mr Wilkinson, a clergyman."

The Lotos-Eaters, of course, is at the opposite pole of the poet's genius. A few plain verses of the *Odyssey*, almost bald in their reticence, are the *point de repère* of the most magical vision expressed in the most musical verse. Here is the languid charm of Spenser, enriched with many classical memories, and pictures of natural beauty gorgeously yet delicately painted. After the excision of some verses, rather fantastical, in 1842, the poem became a flawless masterpiece,—one of the eternal possessions of song.

On the other hand, the opening of *The Dream of Fair Women* was marred in 1833 by the grotesque intro-ductory verses about "a man that sails in a balloon." Young as Tennyson was, these freakish passages are a psychological marvel in the work of one who did not lack the saving sense of humour. The poet, wafted on the wing and "pinion that the Theban eagle bear," cannot conceivably be likened to an aeronaut waving flags out of a balloon—except in a spirit of self-mockery which was not Tennyson's. His remarkable self-discipline in excising the fantastic and superfluous, and reducing his work to its classical perfection of thought and form, is nowhere more remarkable than in this magnificent vision. It is probably by mere accidental coincidence of thought that, in the verses *To J. S.* (James Spedding), Tennyson reproduces the noble speech on the warrior's death which Sir Walter Scott places in the lips of the great Dundee: "It is the memory which the soldier leaves behind him, like the long train of light that follows the sunken sun, *that* is all that is worth caring for," the light which lingers eternally on the hills of Atholl. Tennyson's lines are a close parallel:—

> "His memory long will live alone
> In all our hearts, as mournful light
> That broods above the fallen sun,
> And dwells in heaven half the night."

Though Tennyson disliked the exhibition of "the chips of the workshop," we have commented on them, on the early readings of the early volumes. They may be regarded more properly as the sketches of a master than as "chips," and do more than merely engage the idle curiosity of the fanatics of first editions. They prove that the poet was studious of perfection, and wisely studious, for his alterations, unlike those of some authors, were almost invariably for the better, the saner, the more mature in taste.   The early readings are also worth notice, because they partially explain, by their occasionally fantastic and humourless character, the lack of early and general recognition of the poet's genius.   The native prejudice of mankind is not in favour of a new poet.   Of new poets there are always so many, most of them bad, that nature has protected mankind by an armour of suspiciousness.   The world, and Lockhart, easily found good reasons for distrusting this new claimant of the ivy and the bays : moreover, since about 1814 there had been a reaction against new poetry.   The market was glutted.   Scott had set everybody on reading, and too many on writing, novels. The great reaction of the century against all forms of literature except prose fiction had begun.   Near the very date of Tennyson's first volume Bulwer Lytton, as we saw, had frankly explained that he wrote novels because nobody would look at anything else.   Tennyson had to overcome this universal, or all but universal, indifference to new poetry, and, after being silent for ten years, overcome it he did—a remarkable victory of art and of patient courage.   Times were even worse for poets than to-day.   Three hundred copies of the new volume were sold!   But Tennyson's friends were not puffers in league with pushing publishers.

Meanwhile the poet in 1833 went on quietly and undefeated with his work.   He composed *The Gar-*

dener's Daughter, and was at work on the *Morte d'Arthur*, suppressed till the ninth year, on the Horatian plan. Many poems were produced (and even written out, which a number of his pieces never were), and were left in manuscript till they appeared in the Biography. Most of these are so little worthy of the author that the marvel is how he came to write them— in what uninspired hours. Unlike Wordsworth, he could weed the tares from his wheat. His studies were in Greek, German, Italian, history (a little), and chemistry, botany, and electricity—"cross-grained Muses," these last.

It was on September 15, 1833, that Arthur Hallam died. Unheralded by sign or symptom of disease as it was, the news fell like a thunderbolt from a serene sky. Tennyson's and Hallam's love had been "passing the love of women." A blow like this drives a man on the rocks of the ultimate, the insoluble problems of destiny. "Is this the end?" Nourished as on the milk of lions, on the elevating and strengthening doctrines of popular science, trained from childhood to forego hope and attend evening lectures, the young critics of our generation find Tennyson a weakling because he had hopes and fears concerning the ultimate renewal of what was more than half his life—his friendship.

> "That faith I fain would keep,
>   That hope I'll not forego :
> Eternal be the sleep
>   Unless to waken so,"

wrote Lockhart, and the verses echoed ceaselessly in
the widowed heart of Carlyle. These men, it is part
of the duty of critics later born to remember, were not
children or cowards, though they dreamed, and hoped,
and feared. We ought to make allowance for failings
incident to an age not yet fully enlightened by popular
science, and still undivorced from spiritual ideas that
are as old as the human race, and perhaps not likely
to perish while that race exists. Now and then even
scientific men have been mistaken, especially when
they have declined to examine evidence, as in this
problem of the transcendental nature of the human
spirit they usually do. At all events Tennyson was
unconvinced that death is the end, and shortly after
the fatal tidings arrived from Vienna he began to
write fragments in verse preluding to the poem of
In Memoriam. He also began, in a mood of great
misery, *The Two Voices; or, Thoughts of a Suicide.*
The poem seems to have been partly done by September 1834, when Spedding commented on it, and on
the beautiful *Sir Galahad*, "intended for something of
a male counterpart to *St Agnes.*" The *Morte d'Arthur*
Tennyson then thought "the best thing I have managed lately." Very early in 1835 many stanzas of *In
Memoriam* had taken form. "I do not wish to be
dragged forward in any shape before the reading public
at present," wrote the poet, when he heard that Mill
desired to write on him His *Œnone* he had brought
to its new perfection, and did not desire comments on

work now several years old.   He also wrote his *Ulysses* and his *Tithonus*.

If ever the term "morbid" could have been applied to Tennyson, it would have been in the years immediately following the death of Arthur Hallam.   But the application would have been unjust.   True, the poet was living out of the world; he was unhappy, and he was, as people say, "doing nothing."   He was so poor that he sold his Chancellor's prize gold medal, and he did not

> "Scan his whole horizon
> In quest of what he could clap eyes on,"

in the way of money-making, which another poet describes as the normal attitude of all men as well as of pirates.   A careless observer would have thought that the poet was dawdling.   But he dwelt in no Castle of Indolence; he studied, he composed, he corrected his verses: like Sir Walter in Liddesdale, "he was making himsel' a' the time."   He did not neglect the movements of the great world in that dawn of discontent with the philosophy of commercialism.   But it was not his vocation to plunge into the fray, and on to platforms.

It is a very rare thing anywhere, especially in England, for a man deliberately to choose poetry as the duty of his life, and to remain loyal, as a consequence, to the bride of St Francis—Poverty.   This loyalty Tennyson maintained, even under the tempta-

tion to make money in recognised ways presented by
his new-born love for his future wife, Miss Emily
Sellwood. They had first met in 1830, when she, a
girl of seventeen, seemed to him like "a Dryad or an
Oread wandering here." But admiration became the
affection of a lifetime when Tennyson met Miss
Sellwood as bridesmaid to her sister, the bride of his
brother Charles, in 1836. The poet could not afford
to marry, and, like the hero of *Locksley Hall*, he may
have asked himself, "What is that which I should do?"
By 1840 he had done nothing tangible and lucrative,
and correspondence between the lovers was forbidden.
That neither dreamed of Tennyson's deserting poetry
for a more normal profession proved of great benefit
to the world. The course is one which could only be
justified by the absolute certainty of possessing genius.

III.

1837-1842.

In 1837 the Tennysons left the old rectory; till 1840 they lived at High Beech in Epping Forest, and after a brief stay at Tunbridge Wells went to Boxley, near Maidstone.

It appears that at last the poet had "beat his music out," though his friends "still tried to cheer him." But the man who wrote *Ulysses* when his grief was fresh could not be suspected of declining into a hypochondriac. "If I mean to make my mark at all, it must be by shortness," he said at this time; "for the men before me had been so diffuse, and most of the big things, except *King Arthur*, had been done." The age had not *la tête épique*: Poe had announced the paradox that there is no such thing as a long poem, and even in dealing with Arthur, Tennyson followed the example of Theocritus in writing, not an epic, but epic idylls. Long poems suit an age of listeners, for which they were originally composed, or of leisure and few books. At present epics are read for duty's sake, not for the only valid reason, "for human pleasure," in FitzGerald's phrase.

Between 1838 and 1840 Tennyson made some brief tours in England with FitzGerald, and, coming from Coventry, wrote *Godiva*. His engagement with Miss Sellwood seemed to be adjourned *sine die*, as they were forbidden to correspond.

By 1841 Tennyson was living at Mablethorpe on the Lincolnshire coast; working at his volumes of 1842, much urged by FitzGerald and American admirers, who had heard of the poet through Emerson. Moxon was to be the publisher, himself something of a poet; but early in 1842 he had not yet received the MS. Perhaps Emerson heard of Tennyson through Carlyle, who, says Sterling, "said more in your praise than in any one's except Cromwell, and an American backwoodsman who has killed thirty or forty people with a bowie-knife." Carlyle at this time was much attached to Lockhart, editor of the *Quarterly Review*, and it may have been Carlyle who converted Lockhart to admiration of his old victim. Carlyle had very little more appreciation of Keats than had Byron, or (in early days) Lockhart, and it was probably as much the man of heroic physical mould, "a life-guardsman spoilt by making poetry," and the unaffected companion over a pipe, as the poet, that attracted him in Tennyson. As we saw, when the two triumphant volumes of 1842 did appear, Lockhart asked Sterling to review whatever book he pleased (meaning the Poems) in the *Quarterly*. The praise of Sterling may seem lukewarm to us, especially when compared with that

of Spedding in the *Edinburgh*. But Sterling, and
Lockhart too, were obliged to " gang warily." Lockhart had, to his constant annoyance, " a partner, Mr
Croker," and I have heard from the late Dean Boyle
that Mr Croker was much annoyed by even the mild
applause yielded in the *Quarterly* to the author of
the *Morte d'Arthur*.

While preparing the volumes of 1842 at Boxley,
Tennyson's life was divided between London and the
society of his brother-in-law, Mr Edmund Lushington, the great Greek scholar and Professor of Greek
at Glasgow University. There was in Mr Lushington's
personal aspect, and noble simplicity of manner and
character, something that strongly resembled Tennyson himself. Among their common friends were Lord
Houghton (Monckton Milnes), Mr Lear of the *Book of
Nonsense* ("with such a pencil, such a pen"), Mr
Venables (who at school modified the profile of
Thackeray), and Lord Kelvin. In town Tennyson
met his friends at The Cock, which he rendered classic ;
among them were Thackeray, Forster, Maclise, and
Dickens. The times were stirring : social agitation,
and " Carol philosophy " in Dickens, with growls from
Carlyle, marked the period. There was also a kind of
optimism in the air, a prophetic optimism, not yet
fulfilled.

" Fly, happy happy sails, and bear the Press ! "

That mission no longer strikes us as exquisitely

felicitous. "The mission of the Cross," and of the missionaries, means international complications; and "the markets of the Golden Year" are precisely the most fruitful causes of wars and rumours of wars :—

"Sea and air are dark
With great contrivances of Power."

Tennyson's was not an unmitigated optimism, and had no special confidence in

"The herd, wild hearts and feeble wings
That every sophister can lime."

His political poetry, in fact, was very unlike the socialist chants of Mr William Morris, or *Songs before Sunrise.* He had nothing to say about

"The blood on the hands of the King,
And the lie on the lips of the Priest."

The hands of Presidents have not always been unstained; nor are statements of a mythical nature confined to the lips of the clergy. The poet was anxious that freedom should "broaden down," but "slowly," not with indelicate haste. Persons who are more in a hurry will never care for the political poems, and it is certain that Tennyson did not feel sympathetically inclined towards the Iberian patriot who said that his darling desire was "to cut the throats of all the *curés,*" like some Covenanters of old. "Mais vous connaissez mon cœur"—"and a pretty black one it is," thought young Tennyson. So cautious in youth, during his Pyrenean tour with Hallam in 1830, Tennyson could not become a convinced revolutionary later. We must accept him with his limitations : nor must we confuse him with the hero of his *Locksley Hall*, one of the most popular, and most parodied, of the poems of 1842 : full of beautiful images and " confusions of a wasted youth," a youth dramatically conceived, and in no way auto-biographical.

In so marvellous a treasure of precious things as the volumes of 1842, perhaps none is more splendid, perfect, and perdurable than the *Morte d'Arthur*. It had been written seven years earlier, and pronounced by the poet " not bad." Tennyson was never, perhaps, a very deep Arthurian student. A little cheap copy of Malory was his companion.[1] He does not appear to have gone deeply into the French and German " literature of the subject." Malory's compilation (1485) from French and English sources, with the *Mabinogion* of Lady Charlotte Guest, sufficed for him as materials. The whole poem, enshrined in the memory of all lovers of verse, is richly studded, as the hilt of Excalibur, with classical memories. " A faint Homeric echo " it is not, nor a Virgilian echo, but the absolute voice of old romance, a thing that might have been chanted by

> " The lonely maiden of the Lake "

when

> " Nine years she wrought it, sitting in the deeps,
> Upon the hidden bases of the hills."

---

[1] The writer knew this edition before he knew Tennyson's poems.

Perhaps the most exquisite adaptation of all are the lines
from the *Odyssey*—

"Where falls not hail nor rain, nor any snow."

"Softly through the flutes of the Grecians" came first
these Elysian numbers, then through Lucretius, then
through Tennyson's own *Lucretius*, then in Mr
Swinburne's *Atalanta in Calydon*:—

> "Lands indiscoverable in the unheard-of west
> Round which the strong stream of a sacred sea
> Rolls without wind for ever, and the snow
> There shows not her white wings and windy feet,
> Nor thunder nor swift rain saith anything,
> Nor the sun burns, but all things rest and thrive."

So fortunate in their transmission through poets have
been the lines of "the Ionian father of the rest," the
greatest of them all.

In the variety of excellences which marks Tennyson,
the new English idylls of 1842 hold their prominent
place. Nothing can be more exquisite and more
English than the picture of "the garden that I love."
Theocritus cannot be surpassed; but the idyll matches
to the seventh of his, where it is most closely followed,
and possesses such a picture of a girl as the Sicilian
never tried to paint.

Dora is another idyll, resembling the work of a
Wordsworth in a clime softer than that of the Fells. The
lays of Edwin Morris and Edward Bull are not among

the more enduring of even the playful poems. The
St Simeon Stylites appears "made to the hand" of the
author of *Men and Women* rather than of Tennyson.
The grotesque vanity of the anchorite is so remote
from us, that we can scarcely judge of the truth of
the picture, though the East has still her parallels to
St Simeon. From the almost, perhaps quite, incred-
ible ascetic the poet lightly turns to "society verse"
lifted up into the air of poetry, in the charm of *The
Talking Oak*, and the happy flitting sketches of actual
history; and thence to the strength and passion of
Love and Duty. Shall

"Sin itself be found
The cloudy porch oft opening on the Sun?"

That this is the province of sin is a pretty popular
modern moral. But Honour is the better part, and here
was a poet who had the courage to say so; though, to
be sure, the words ring strange in an age when highly
respectable matrons assure us that "passion," like
charity, covers a multitude of sins. *Love and Duty*, we
must admit, is "early Victorian."

The *Ulysses* is almost a rival to the *Morte d'Arthur.*
It is of an early date, after Arthur Hallam's death, and
Thackeray speaks of the poet chanting his

"Great Achilles whom we knew,"

as if he thought that this was in Cambridge days.
But it is later than these. Tennyson said, "*Ulysses*

was written soon after Arthur Hallam's death, and
gave my feeling about the need of going forward, and
braving the struggle of life, perhaps more simply than
anything in *In Memoriam*." Assuredly the expression
is more simple, and more noble, and the personal
emotion more dignified for the classic veil. When
the plaintive Pessimist ("'proud of the title,' as the
Living Skeleton said when they showed him") tells us
that "not to have been born is best," we may answer
with Ulysses—

> " Life piled on life
> Were all too little."

The Ulysses of Tennyson, of course, is Dante's Ulysses,
not Homer's Odysseus, who brought home to Ithaca
not one of his mariners. His last known adventure,
the journey to the land of men who knew not the
savour of salt, Odysseus was to make on foot and
alone; so spake the ghost of Tiresias within the poplar
pale of Persephone.

The Two Voices expresses the contest of doubts and
griefs with the spirit of endurance and joy which speaks
alone in *Ulysses*. The man who is unhappy, but does
not want to put an end to himself, has certainly the
better of the argument with the despairing Voice. The
arguments of " that barren Voice " are, indeed, remark-
ably deficient in cogency and logic, if we can bring
ourselves to strip the discussion of its poetry. The
original title, *Thoughts of a Suicide*, was inappropriate.
The suicidal suggestions are promptly faced and con-

futed, and the mood of the author is throughout that of one who thinks life worth living :—

> " Whatever crazy sorrow saith,
>   No life that breathes with human breath
>   Has ever truly long'd for death.
>
>   'Tis life whereof our nerves are scant,
>   Oh life, not death, for which we pant ;
>   More life, and fuller, that I want."

This appears to be a satisfactory reply to the persons who eke out a livelihood by publishing pessimistic books, and hooting, as the great Alexandre Dumas says, at the great drama of Life.

With *The Day-Dream* (of The Sleeping Beauty) Tennyson again displays his matchless range of powers. Verse of Society rises into a charmed and musical fantasy, passing from the Berlin - wool work of the period

> (" Take the broidery frame, and add
>   A crimson to the quaint Macaw ")

into the enchanted land of the fable : princes immortal, princesses eternally young and fair. The *St Agnes* and *Sir Galahad*, companion pieces, contain the romance, as *St Simeon Stylites* shows the repulsive side of asceticism ; for the saint and the knight are young, beautiful, and eager as St Theresa in her childhood. It has been said, I do not know on what authority, that the poet had no recollection of composing *Sir Galahad*, any more than Scott remembered composing *The Bride of Lammermoor*, or Thackeray parts of *Pendennis*. The haunting of Tennyson's mind by the Arthurian legends prompted also the lovely fragment on the Queen's last Maying, *Sir Launcelot and Queen Guinevere*, a thing of perfect charm and music. The ballads of *Lady Clare* and *The Lord of Burleigh* are not examples of the poet in his strength ; for his power and fantasy we must turn to *The Vision of Sin*, where the early passages have the languid voluptuous music of *The Lotos-Eaters*, with the ethical element superadded, while the portion beginning—

"Wrinkled ostler, grim and thin !"

is in parts reminiscent of Burns's *Jolly Beggars*. In *Break, Break, Break*, we hear a note prelusive to *In Memoriam*, much of which was already composed.

The Poems of 1842 are always vocal in the memories of all readers of English verse. None are more familiar, at least to men of the generations which immediately followed Tennyson's. FitzGerald was apt to think that the poet never again attained the same level, and I venture to suppose that he never rose above it. For FitzGerald's opinion, right or wrong, it is easy to account. He had seen all the pieces in manuscript; they were his cherished possession before the world knew them. *C'est mon homme*, he might have said of Tennyson, as Boileau said of Molière. Before the public awoke FitzGerald had "discovered Tennyson," and that at the age most open to poetry and most enthusiastic in friendship. Again, the Poems of 1842 were *short*, while *The Princess*, *Maud*, and *The Idylls of the King* were relatively long, and, with *In Memoriam*, possessed unity of subject. They lacked the rich, the unexampled variety of topic, treatment, and theme which marks the Poems of 1842. These were all reasons why FitzGerald should think that the two slim green volumes held the poet's work at its highest level. Perhaps he was not wrong, after all.

IV.

1842-1848—*THE PRINCESS.*

THE Poems, and such criticisms as those of Spedding and Sterling, gave Tennyson his place. All the world of letters heard of him. Dean Bradley tells us how he took Oxford by storm in the days of the undergraduateship of Clough and Matthew Arnold. Probably both of these young writers did not share the undergraduate enthusiasm. Mr Arnold, we know, did not reckon Tennyson *un esprit puissant.* Like Wordsworth (who thought Tennyson "decidedly the first of our living poets, . . . he has expressed in the strongest terms his gratitude to my writings"), Arnold was no fervent admirer of his contemporaries. Besides, if Tennyson's work is "a criticism of Life," the moral criticism, so far, was hidden in flowers, like the sword of Aristogiton at the feast. But, on the whole, Tennyson had won the young men who cared for poetry, though Sir Robert Peel had never heard of him: and to win the young, as Theocritus desired to do, is more than half the battle. On September 8, 1842, the poet was able to tell Mr Lushington that "500 of my books are sold; according to Moxon's brother, I have made a sensation." The sales were not like those of *Childe Harold* or *Marmion;* but for some twenty years new poetry had not sold at all. Novels had come in about 1814, and few wanted or bought recent verse. But Carlyle was converted. He spoke no more of a spoiled guardsman. "If you knew what my relation has been to the thing called 'English Poetry' for many years back, you would think such a fact" (his pleasure in the book) "surprising." Carlyle had been living (as Mrs Carlyle too well knew) in Oliver Cromwell, a hero who probably took no delight in *Lycidas* or *Comus*, in Lovelace or Carew. "I would give all my poetry to have made one song like that," said Tennyson of Lovelace's *Althea*. But Noll would have disregarded them all alike, and Carlyle was full of the spirit of the Protector. To conquer him was indeed a victory for Tennyson; while Dickens, not a reading man, expressed his " earnest and sincere homage."

But Tennyson was not successful in the modern way. Nobody " interviewed " him. His photograph, of course, with disquisitions on his pipes and slippers, did not adorn the literary press. His literary income was not magnified by penny-a-liners. He did not become a lion; he never would roar and shake his mane in drawing-rooms. Lockhart held that Society was the most agreeable form of the stage: the dresses and actresses incomparably the prettiest. But Tennyson

liked Society no better than did General Gordon.   He
had friends enough, and no desire for new acquaintances.   Indeed, his fortune was shattered at this time
by a strange investment in wood-carving by machinery.
Ruskin had only just begun to write, and wood-carving
by machinery was still deemed an enterprise at once
philanthropic and æsthetic.   " My father's worldly
goods were all gone," says Lord Tennyson.   The
poet's health suffered extremely : he tried a fashionable " cure " at Cheltenham, where he saw miracles of
healing, but underwent none.   In September 1845
Peel was moved by Lord Houghton to recommend
the poet for a pension (£200 annually).   " I have
done nothing slavish to get it : I never even solicited
for it either by myself or others."   Like Dr Johnson,
he honourably accepted what was offered in honour.
For some reason many persons who write in the press
are always maddened when such good fortune, however small, however well merited, falls to a brother
in letters.   They, of course, were " causelessly bitter."
" Let them rave ! "

If few of the rewards of literary success arrived, the
penalties at once began, and only ceased with the poet's
existence.   " If you only knew what a nuisance these
volumes of verse are !   Rascals send me theirs per
post from America, and I have more than once been
knocked up out of bed to pay three or four shillings for
books of which I can't get through one page, for of all
books the most insipid reading is second-rate verse."

Would that versifiers took the warning! Tennyson had not sent his little firstlings to Coleridge and Wordsworth: they are only the hopeless rhymers who bombard men of letters with their lyrics and tragedies.

Mr Browning was a sufferer. To one young twitterer he replied in the usual way. The bard wrote acknowledging the letter, but asking for a definite criticism. "I do not think myself a Shakespeare or a Milton, but I *know* I am better than Mr Coventry Patmore or Mr Austin Dobson." Mr Browning tried to procrastinate: he was already deeply engaged with earlier arrivals of volumes of song. The poet was hurt, not angry; he had expected other things from Mr Browning: *he* ought to know his duty to youth. At the intercession of a relation Mr Browning now did his best, and the minstrel, satisfied at last, repeated his conviction of his superiority to the authors of *The Angel in the House* and *Beau Brocade*. Probably no man, not even Mr Gladstone, ever suffered so much from minstrels as Tennyson. He did not suffer them gladly.

In. 1846 the Poems reached their fourth edition. Sir Edward Bulwer Lytton (bitten by what fly who knows?) attacked Tennyson in *The New Timon*, a forgotten satire. We do not understand the ways of that generation. The cheap and spiteful *genre* of satire, with its forged morality, its sham indignation, its appeal to the ape-like passions, has gone out. Lytton had suffered many things (not in verse) from Jeames Yellowplush: I do not know that he hit back at Thackeray, but he "passed it on" to Thackeray's old college companion. Tennyson, for once, replied (in *Punch :* the verses were sent thither by John Forster) ; the answer was one of magnificent contempt. But he soon decided that

> " The noblest answer unto such
>   Is perfect stillness when they brawl."

Long afterwards the poet dedicated a work to the son of Lord Lytton. He replied to no more satirists.[1] Our difficulty, of course, is to conceive such an attack coming from a man of Lytton's position and genius. He was no hungry hack, and could, and did, do infinitely better things than "stand in a false following" of Pope. Probably Lytton had a false idea that Tennyson was a rich man, a branch of his family being affluent, and so resented the little pension. The poet was so far from rich in 1846, and even after the publication of *The Princess*, that his marriage had still to be deferred for four years.

On reading *The Princess* afresh one is impressed, despite old familiarity, with the extraordinary influence of its beauty. Here are, indeed, the best words best placed, and that curious felicity of style which makes every line a marvel, and an eternal possession. It is as if Tennyson had taken the advice which Keats gave to Shelley, "Load every rift with ore." To choose but

---

[1] The author of the spiteful letters was an unpublished anonymous person.

one or two examples, how the purest and freshest
impression of nature is re-created in mind and memory
by the picture of Melissa with

> " All her thoughts as fair within her eyes,
> As bottom agates seen to wave and float
> In crystal currents of clear morning seas."

The lyric, " Tears, idle tears," is far beyond praise :
once read it seems like a thing that has always existed
in the world of poetic archetypes, and has now been
not so much composed as discovered and revealed.
The many pictures and similitudes in *The Princess*
have a magical gorgeousness :—

> " From the illumined hall
> Long lanes of splendour slanted o'er a press
> Of snowy shoulders, thick as herded ewes,
> And rainbow robes, and gems and gem-like eyes,
> And gold and golden heads ; they to and fro
> Fluctuated, as flowers in storm, some red, some pale."

The " small sweet Idyll " from

> " A volume of the poets of her land "

is pure Theocritus. It has been admirably rendered
into Greek by Mr Gilbert Murray. The exquisite
beauties of style are not less exquisitely blended in
the confusions of a dream, for a dream is the thing
most akin to *The Princess*. Time does not exist in
the realm of Gama, or in the ideal university of Ida.
We have a bookless North, severed but by a frontier

pillar from a golden and learned South. The arts,
from architecture to miniature - painting, are in their
highest perfection, while knights still tourney in armour,
and the quarrel of two nations is decided as in the
gentle and joyous passage of arms at Ashby de la
Zouche. Such confusions are purposefully dream-like :
the vision being a composite thing, as dreams are,
haunted by the modern scene of the holiday in the
park, the "gallant glorious chronicle," the Abbey, and
that "old crusading knight austere," Sir Ralph. The
seven narrators of the scheme are like the "split
personalities" of dreams, and the whole scheme is of
great technical skill. The earlier editions lacked the
beautiful songs of the ladies, and that additional trait of
dream, the strange trance-like seizures of the Prince :
"fallings from us, vanishings," in Wordsworthian
phrase ; instances of "dissociation," in modern psychological terminology. Tennyson himself, like Shelley
and Wordsworth, had experience of this kind of
dreaming awake which he attributes to his Prince, to
strengthen the shadowy yet brilliant character of his
romance. It is a thing of normal and natural *points de
repère ;* of daylight suggestion, touched as with the mag-
nifying and intensifying elements of haschish-begotten
phantasmagoria. In the same way opium raised into the
region of brilliant vision that passage of Purchas which
Coleridge was reading before he dreamed *Kubla Khan.*
But in Tennyson the effects were deliberately sought and
secured.

One might conjecture, though Lord Tennyson says nothing on the subject, that among the suggestions for *The Princess* was the opening of *Love's Labour's Lost.* Here the King of Navarre devises the College of Recluses, which is broken up by the arrival of the Princess of France, Rosaline, and the other ladies :—

King. Our Court shall be a little Academe,
Still and contemplative in living art.
You three, Biron, Dumain, and Longaville,
Have sworn for three years' term to live with me,
My fellow-scholars, and to keep those statutes.

.   .   .   .

Biron. That is, to live and study here three years.
But there are other strict observances ;
As, not to see a woman in that term.

.   .   .   .

[*Reads*] 'That no woman shall come within a mile of my Court :' Hath this been proclaimed ?
Long. Four days ago.
Biron. Let's see the penalty. [*Reads*] 'On pain of losing her tongue.'

The Princess then arrives with her ladies, as the Prince does with Cyril and Florian, as Charles did, with Buckingham, in Spain. The conclusion of Shakespeare is Tennyson's conclusion—

" We cannot cross the cause why we are born."

The later poet reverses the attitude of the sexes in *Love's Labour's Lost:* it is the women who make and break the vow ; and the women in *The Princess* insist on the " grand, epic, homicidal " scenes, while the men are debarred, more or less, from a sportive treatment of the subject. The tavern catch of Cyril; the laughable pursuit of the Prince by the feminine Proctors; the draggled appearance of the adventurers in female garb, are concessions to the humour of the situation. Shakespeare would certainly have given us the song of Cyril at the picnic, and comic enough the effect would have been on the stage. It may be a gross employment, but *The Princess*, with the pretty chorus of girl undergraduates,

" In colours gayer than the morning mist,"

went reasonably well in opera. Merely considered as a romantic fiction, *The Princess* presents higher proofs of original narrative genius than any other such attempt by its author.

The poem is far from being deficient in that human interest which Shelley said that it was as vain to ask from *him*, as to seek to buy a leg of mutton at a gin-shop. The characters, the protagonists, with Cyril, Melissa, Lady Blanche, the child Aglaia, King Gama, the other king, Arac, and the hero's mother—beautifully studied from the mother of the poet—are all sufficiently human. But they seem to waver in the magic air, "as all the golden autumn woodland reels" athwart the fires of autumn leaves. For these reasons, and because of the designed fantasy of the whole composition, *The Princess* is essentially a poem for the true lovers of poetry, of Spenser and of Coleridge. The serious motive, the question of Woman, her wrongs, her rights, her education, her capabilities, was not "in the air" in 1847. To be sure it had often been "in the air." The Alexandrian Platonists, the Renaissance, even the age of Anne, had their emancipated and learned ladies. Early Greece had Sappho, Corinna, and Erinna, the first the chief of lyric poets, even in her fragments, the two others applauded by all Hellas. The French Revolution had begotten Mary Wollstone-craft Godwin and her *Vindication of the Rights of Women*, and in France George Sand was prominent and emancipated enough while the poet wrote. But, the question of love apart, George Sand was "very, very woman," shining as a domestic character and fond of needlework. England was not excited about the question which has since produced so many disputants, inevitably shrill, and has not been greatly meddled with by women of genius, George Eliot or Mrs Oliphant. The poem, in the public indifference as to feminine education, came rather prematurely. We have now ladies' colleges, not in haunts remote from man, but by the sedged banks of Cam and Cherwell. There have been no revolutionary results : no boys have spied these chaste nests, with echoing romantic consequences. The beauty and splendour of the Princess's university have not arisen in light and colour, and it is only at St Andrews that girls wear the academic and becoming costume of the scarlet gown. The real is far below the ideal, but the real in 1847 seemed eminently remote, or even impossible.

The learned Princess herself was not on our level as to knowledge and the past of womankind. She knew not of their masterly position in the law of ancient Egypt. Gynæcocracy and matriarchy, the woman the head of the savage or prehistoric group, were things hidden from her. She "glanced at the Lycian custom," but not at the Pictish, a custom which would have suited George Sand to a marvel. She maligned the Hottentots.

> "The highest is the measure of the man,
> And not the Kaffir, Hottentot, Malay."

The Hottentots had long ago anticipated the Princess and her shrill modern sisterhood. If we take the Greeks, or even ourselves, we may say, with Dampier (1689), "The Hodmadods, though a nasty people, yet are gentlemen to these" as regards the position of women. Let us hear Mr Hartland : " In every Hottentot's house the wife is supreme. Her husband, poor fellow, though he may wield wide power and influence out of doors, at home dare not even take a mouthful of sour-milk out of the household vat without her permission. . . . The highest oath a man can take is to swear by his eldest sister, and if he abuses this name he forfeits to her his finest goods and sheep."

However, in 1847 England had not yet thought of imitating the Hodmadods. Consequently, and by reason of the purely literary and elaborately fantastical character of *The Princess*, it was not of a nature to increase the poet's fame and success. "My book is out, and I hate it, and so no doubt will you," Tennyson wrote to FitzGerald, who hated it and said so. "Like Carlyle, I gave up all hopes of him after *The Princess ;*" indeed it was not apt to conciliate Carlyle. "None of the songs had the old champagne flavour," said Fitz ; and Lord Tennyson adds, "Nothing either by Thackeray or by my father met FitzGerald's approbation unless he had first seen it in manuscript." This prejudice was very human. Lord Tennyson remarks, as to the poet's meaning in this work, born too early, that "the sooner woman finds out, before the great educational movement begins, that 'woman is not undeveloped man, but diverse,' the better it will be for the progress of the world."

But probably the "educational movement" will not make much difference to womankind on the whole. The old Platonic remark that woman "does the same things as man, but not so well," will eternally hold good, at least in the arts, and in letters, except in rare cases of genius. A new Jeanne d'Arc, the most signal example of absolute genius in history, will not come again ; and the ages have waited vainly for a new Sappho or a new Jane Austen. Literature, poetry, painting, have always been fields open to woman. But two names exhaust the roll of women of the highest rank in letters—Sappho and Jane Austen. And "when did woman ever yet invent ?" In "arts of government" Elizabeth had courage, and just saving sense enough to

yield to Cecil at the eleventh hour, and escape the fate
of "her sister and her foe," the beautiful unhappy queen
who told her ladies that she dared to look on whatever
men dared to do, and herself would do it if her strength
so served her."[1]   "The foundress of the Babylonian
walls" is a myth; "the Rhodope that built the Pyra-
mid" is not a creditable myth; for exceptions to Knox's
"Monstrous Regiment of Women" we must fall back
on "The Palmyrene that fought Aurelian," and the
revered name of the greatest of English queens, Victoria.
Thus history does not encourage the hope that a man-
like education will raise many women to the level of
the highest of their sex in the past, or even that the
enormous majority of women will take advantage of the
opportunity of a man-like education.   A glance at the
numerous periodicals designed for the reading of women
depresses optimism, and the Princess's prophecy of

> "Two plummets dropped for one to sound the abyss
> Of science, and the secrets of the mind,"

is not near fulfilment.   Fortunately the sex does not "love
the Metaphysics," and perhaps has not yet produced even
a manual of Logic.   It must suffice man and woman to

> "Walk this world
> Yoked in all exercise of noble end,"

of a more practical character, while woman is at liberty

> "To live and learn and be
> All that not harms distinctive womanhood."

---

[1] The Lennox MSS.

This was the conclusion of the poet who had the most chivalrous reverence for womanhood. This is the *eirenicon* of that old strife between the women and the men—that war in which both armies are captured. It may not be acceptable to excited lady combatants, who think man their foe, when the real enemy is (what Porson damned) the Nature of Things.

A new poem like *The Princess* would soon reach the public of our day, so greatly increased are the uses of advertisement. But *The Princess* moved slowly from edition to revised and improved edition, bringing neither money nor much increase of fame. The poet was living with his family at Cheltenham, where among his new acquaintances were Sydney Dobell, the poet of a few exquisite pieces, and F. W. Robertson, later so popular as a preacher at Brighton. Meeting him for the first time, and knowing Robertson's "wish to pluck the heart from my mystery, from pure nervousness I would only talk of beer." This kind of shyness beset Tennyson. A lady tells me that as a girl (and a very beautiful girl) she and her sister, and a third, *nec diversa*, met the poet, and expected high discourse. But his speech was all of that wingless insect which "gets there, all the same," according to an American lyrist ; the insect which fills Mrs Carlyle's letters with bulletins of her success or failure in domestic campaigns.

Tennyson kept visiting London, where he saw Thackeray and the despair of Carlyle, and at Bath

House he was too modest to be introduced to the
great Duke whose requiem he was to sing so nobly.
Oddly enough Douglas Jerrold enthusiastically assured
Tennyson, at a dinner of a Society of Authors, that
"you are the one who will live." To that end,
humanly speaking, he placed himself under the celebrated Dr Gully and his "water-cure," a foible
of that period. In 1848 he made a tour to King
Arthur's Cornish bounds, and another to Scotland,
where the Pass of Brander disappointed him : perhaps
he saw it on a fine day, and, like Glencoe, it needs
tempest and mist lit up by the white fires of many
waterfalls. By bonny Doon he "fell into a passion of
tears," for he had all of Keats's sentiment for Burns :
"There never was immortal poet if he be not one."
Of all English poets, the warmest in the praise of Burns
have been the two most unlike himself—Tennyson and
Keats. It was the songs that Tennyson preferred ;
Wordsworth .liked the *Cottar's Saturday Night*.

61

V.

IN MEMORIAM.

IN May 1850 a few copies of *In Memoriam* were printed for friends, and presently the poem was published without author's name. The pieces had been composed at intervals, from 1833 onwards. It is to be observed that the " section about evolution " was written some years before 1844, when the ingenious hypotheses of Robert Chambers, in *Vestiges of Creation*, were given to the world, and caused a good deal of talk. Ten years, again, after *In Memoriam*, came Darwin's *Origin of Species*. These dates are worth observing. The theory of evolution, of course in a rude mythical shape, is at least as old as the theory of creation, and is found among the speculations of the most backward savages. The Arunta of Central Australia, a race remote from the polite, have a hypothesis of evolution which postulates only a few rudimentary forms of life, a marine environment, and the minimum of supernormal assistance in the way of stimulating the primal forms in the direction of more highly differentiated developments.

"The rudimentary forms, *Inapertwa*, were in reality stages in the transformation of various plants and animals into human beings. . . . They had no distinct limbs or organs of sight, hearing, or smell." They existed in a kind of lumps, and were set free from the cauls which enveloped them by two beings called Ungambikula, "a word which means 'out of nothing,' or 'self-existing.' Men descend from lower animals thus evolved."[1]

This example of the doctrine of evolution in an early shape is only mentioned to prove that the idea has been familiar to the human mind from the lowest known stage of culture. Not less familiar has been the theory of creation by a kind of supreme being. The notion of creation, however, up to 1860, held the foremost place in modern European belief. But Lamarck, the elder Darwin, Monboddo, and others had submitted hypotheses of evolution. Now it was part of the originality of Tennyson, as a philosophic poet, that he had brooded from boyhood on these early theories of evolution, in an age when they were practically unknown to the literary, and were not patronised by the scientific, world. In November 1844 he wrote to Mr Moxon, "I want you to get me a book which I see advertised in the *Examiner:* it seems to contain many speculations with which I have been familiar for years, and on which I have written more than one poem." This book was *Vestiges of Creation.* These

[1] Spencer and Gillen, *Natives of Central Australia*, pp. 388, 389.

poems are the stanzas in *In Memoriam* about "the greater ape," and about Nature as careless of the type : "all shall go." The poetic and philosophic originality of Tennyson thus faced the popular inferences as to the effect of the doctrine of evolution upon religious beliefs long before the world was moved in all its deeps by Darwin's *Origin of Species*. Thus the geological record is inconsistent, we learned, with the record of the first chapters of Genesis. If man is a differentiated monkey, and if a monkey has no soul, or future life (which is taken for granted), where are man's title-deeds to these possessions ? With other difficulties of an obvious kind, these presented themselves to the poet with renewed force when his only chance of happiness depended on being able to believe in a future life, and reunion with the beloved dead. Unbelief had always existed. We hear of atheists in the *Rig Veda*. In the early eighteenth century, in the age of Swift—

> " Men proved, as sure as God's in Gloucester,
>   That Moses was a great impostor."

This distrust of Moses increased with the increase of hypotheses of evolution. But what English poet, before Tennyson, ever attempted "to lay the spectres of the mind "; ever faced world-old problems in their most recent aspects ? I am not acquainted with any poet who attempted this task, and, whatever we may think of Tennyson's success, I do not see how we can deny his originality.

Mr Frederic Harrison, however, thinks that neither "the theology nor the philosophy of *In Memoriam* are new, original, with an independent force and depth of their own." "They are exquisitely graceful re-statements of the theology of the Broad Churchman of the school of F. D. Maurice and Jowett—a combination of Maurice's somewhat illogical piety with Jowett's philosophy of mystification." The piety of Maurice may be as illogical as that of Positivism is logical, and the philosophy of the Master of Balliol may be whatever Mr Harrison pleases to call it. But as Jowett's earliest work (except an essay on Etruscan religion) is of 1855, one does not see how it could influence Tennyson before 1844. And what had the Duke of Argyll written on these themes some years before 1844? The late Duke, to whom Mr Harrison refers in this connection, was born in 1823. His philosophic ideas, if they were to influence Tennyson's *In Memoriam*, must have been set forth by him at the tender age of seventeen, or thereabouts. Mr Harrison's sentence is, "But does *In Memoriam* teach anything, or transfigure any idea which was not about that time" (the time of writing was mainly 1833-1840) "common form with F. D. Maurice, with Jowett, C. Kingsley, F. Robertson, Stopford Brooke, Mr Ruskin, and the Duke of Argyll, Bishops Westcott and Boyd Carpenter?"

The dates answer Mr Harrison. Jowett did not publish anything till at least fifteen years after Tennyson wrote his poems on evolution and belief. Dr Boyd

Carpenter's works previous to 1840 are unknown to bibliography. F. W. Robertson was a young parson at Cheltenham. Ruskin had not published the first volume of *Modern Painters.* His Oxford prize poem is of 1839. Mr Stopford Brooke was at school. The Duke of Argyll was being privately educated : and so with the rest, except the contemporary Maurice. How can Mr Harrison say that, in the time of *In Memoriam,* Tennyson was " in touch with the ideas of Herschel, Owen, Huxley, Darwin, and Tyndall "?[1] When Tennyson wrote the parts of *In Memoriam* which deal with science, nobody beyond their families and friends had heard of Huxley, Darwin, and Tyndall. They had not developed, much less had they published, their "general ideas." Even in his journal of the *Cruise of the Beagle* Darwin's ideas were religious, and he naïvely admired the works of God. It is strange that Mr Harrison has based his criticism, and his theory of Tennyson's want of originality, on what seems to be a historical error. He cites parts of *In Memoriam,* and remarks, " No one can deny that all this is exquisitely beautiful ; that these eternal problems have never been clad in such inimitable grace. . . . But the train of thought is essentially that with which ordinary English readers have been made familiar by F. D. Maurice, Professor Jowett, *Ecce Homo,* *Hypatia,* and now by Arthur Balfour, Mr Drummond, and many valiant companies of *Septem* [why *Septem ?*] *contra*

[1] *Tennyson, Ruskin, and Mill,* pp. 11, 12.

E

Diabolum." One must keep repeating the historical verity that the ideas of *In Memoriam* could not have been "made familiar by" authors who had not yet published anything, or by books yet undreamed of and unborn, such as *Ecce Homo* and Jowett's work on some of St Paul's Epistles. If these books contain the ideas of *In Memoriam*, it is by dint of repetition and borrowing from *In Memoriam*, or by coincidence. The originality was Tennyson's, for we cannot dispute the evidence of dates.

When one speaks of "originality" one does not mean that Tennyson discovered the existence of the ultimate problems. But at Cambridge (1828-1830) he had voted "No" in answer to the question discussed by "the Apostles," "Is an intelligible [intelligent?] First Cause deducible from the phenomena of the universe?"[1] He had also propounded the theory that "the development of the human body might possibly be traced from the radiated vermicular molluscous and vertebrate organisms," thirty years before Darwin published *The Origin of Species*. To be concerned so early with such hypotheses, and to face, in poetry, the religious or irreligious inferences which may be drawn from them, decidedly constitutes part of the poetic originality of Tennyson. His attitude, as a poet, towards religious doubt is only so far not original, as it is part of the general reaction from the freethinking of the eighteenth century. Men had then been freethinkers *avec délices*.

[1] *Life*, p. 37, 1899.

It was a joyous thing to be an atheist, or something very like one; at all events, it was glorious to be "emancipated." Many still find it glorious, as we read in the tone of Mr Huxley, when he triumphs and tramples over pious dukes and bishops. Shelley said that a certain schoolgirl "would make a dear little atheist." But by 1828-1830 men were less joyous in their escape from all that had hitherto consoled and fortified humanity. Long before he dreamed of *In Memoriam*, in the *Poems chiefly Lyrical* of 1830 Tennyson had written—

> "'Yet,' said I, in my morn of youth,
> The unsunn'd freshness of my strength,
> When I went forth in quest of truth,
> 'It is man's privilege to doubt.' . . .
>   Ay me! I fear
> All may not doubt, but everywhere
> Some must clasp Idols. Yet, my God,
> Whom call I Idol? Let Thy dove
> Shadow me over, and my sins
> Be unremember'd, and Thy love
> Enlighten me. Oh teach me yet
> Somewhat before the heavy clod
> Weighs on me, and the busy fret
> Of that sharp-headed worm begins
> In the gross blackness underneath.
>
> Oh weary life! oh weary death!
> Oh spirit and heart made desolate!
> Oh damnèd vacillating state!"

Now the philosophy of *In Memoriam* may be, indeed is, regarded by robust, first-rate, and far from

sensitive minds, as a "damnèd vacillating state."
The poet is not so imbued with the spirit of popular
science as to be sure that he knows everything : knows
that there is nothing but atoms and ether, with no
room for God or a soul. He is far from that
happy cock-certainty, and consequently is exposed to
the contempt of the cock-certain. The poem, says Mr
Harrison, "has made Tennyson the idol of the
Anglican clergyman—the world in which he was born
and the world in which his life was ideally passed—the
idol of all cultured youth and of all æsthetic women.
It is an honourable post to fill"—that of idol. "The
argument of *In Memoriam* apparently is . . . that we
should faintly trust the larger hope." That, I think,
is not the argument, not the conclusion of the poem,
but is a casual expression of one mood among many
moods.

The argument and conclusion of *In Memoriam* are the
argument and conclusion of the life of Tennyson, and of
the love of Tennyson, that immortal passion which was
a part of himself, and which, if aught of us endure, is
living yet, and must live eternally. From the record of
his Life by his son we know that his trust in "the larger
hope" was not "faint," but strengthened with the years.
There are said to have been less hopeful intervals.

His faith is, of course, no argument for others,—at
least it ought not to be. We are all the creatures
of our bias, our environment, our experience, our
emotions. The experience of Tennyson was unlike

the experience of most men. It yielded him subjective grounds for belief. He "opened a path unto
many," like Yama, the Vedic being who discovered
the way to death. But Tennyson's path led not to
death, but to life spiritual, and to hope, and he did
"give a new impulse to the thought of his age," as
other great poets have done. Of course it may be
an impulse to wrong thought. As the philosophical
Australian black said, "We shall know when we are
dead."

Mr Harrison argues as if, unlike Tennyson, Byron,
Wordsworth, Shelley, and Burns produced "original
ideas fresh from their own spirit, and not derived
from contemporary thinkers." I do not know what
original ideas these great poets discovered and pro-
mulgated ; their ideas seem to have been "in the air."
These poets "made them current coin." Shelley
thought that he owed many of his ideas to Godwin,
a contemporary thinker. Wordsworth has a debt to
Plato, a thinker not contemporary. Burns's democratic
independence was "in the air," and had been, in
Scotland, since Elder remarked on it in a letter to
Ingles in 1515. It is not the ideas, it is the expression of the ideas, that marks the poet. Tennyson's
ideas are relatively novel, though as old as Plotinus,
for they are applied to a novel, or at least an un-
familiar, mental situation. Doubt was abroad, as
it always is ; but, for perhaps the first time since
Porphyry wrote his letter to Abammon, the doubters

desired to believe, and said, "Lord, help Thou my unbelief." To robust, not sensitive minds, very much in unity with themselves, the attitude seems contemptible, or at best decently futile. Yet I cannot think it below the dignity of mankind, conscious that it is not omniscient. The poet does fail in logic (*In Memoriam*, cxx.) when he says—

> "Let him, the wiser man who springs
> Hereafter, up from childhood shape
> His action like the greater ape,
> But I was *born* to other things."

I am not well acquainted with the habits of the greater ape, but it would probably be unwise, and perhaps indecent, to imitate him, even if "we also are his offspring." We might as well revert to polyandry and paint, because our Celtic or Pictish ancestors, if we had any, practised the one and wore the other. However, petulances like the verse on the greater ape are rare in *In Memoriam*. To declare that "I would not stay" in life if science proves us to be "cunning casts in clay," is beneath the courage of the Stoical philosophy.

Theologically, the poem represents the struggle with doubts and hopes and fears, which had been with Tennyson from his boyhood, as is proved by the volume of 1830. But the doubts had exerted, probably, but little influence on his happiness till the sudden stroke of loss made life for a time seem almost unbearable unless the doubts were solved. They *were* solved, or stoically set aside, in the *Ulysses*, written in the freshness of grief, with the conclusion that we must be

> "Strong in will
> To strive, to seek, to find, and not to yield."

But the gnawing of grief till it becomes a physical pain, the fever fits of sorrow, the aching *desiderium*, bring back in many guises the old questions. These require new attempts at answers, and are answered, "the sad mechanic exercise" of verse allaying the pain. This is the genesis of *In Memoriam*, not originally written for publication but produced at last as a monument to friendship, and as a book of consolation.

No books of consolation can console except by sympathy; and in *In Memoriam* sympathy and relief have been found, and will be found, by many. Another, we feel, has trodden our dark and stony path, has been shadowed by the shapes of dread which haunt our valley of tribulation : a mind almost infinitely greater than ours has been our fellow - sufferer. He has emerged from the darkness of the shadow of death into the light, whither, as it seems to us, we can scarcely hope to come. It is the sympathy and the example, I think, not the speculations, mystical or scientific, which make *In Memoriam*, in more than name, a book of consolation : even in hours of the sharpest distress, when its technical beauties and wonderful pictures seem shadowy and unreal, like the

yellow sunshine and the woods of that autumn day
when a man learned that his friend was dead. No,
it was not the speculations and arguments that consoled or encouraged us. We did not listen to Tennyson as to Mr Frederic Harrison's glorified Anglican
clergyman. We could not murmur, like the Queen
of the May—

"That good man, the Laureate, has told us words of peace."

What we valued was the poet's companionship.
There was a young reader to whom *All along the
Valley* came as a new poem in a time of recent
sorrow.

" The two-and-thirty years were a mist that rolls away,"

said the singer of *In Memoriam*, and in that hour it
seemed as if none could endure for two-and-thirty
years the companionship of loss. But the years have
gone by, and have left

> " Ever young the face that dwells
> With reason cloister'd in the brain." [1]

In this way to many *In Memoriam* is almost a life-long
companion : we walk with Great - heart for our guide
through the valley Perilous.

In this respect *In Memoriam* is unique, for neither
to its praise nor dispraise is it to be compared with the
other famous elegies of the world. These are brief out-

---

[1] Poem omitted from *In Memoriam*. *Life*, p. 257, 1899.

bursts of grief—real, as in the hopeless words of Catullus over his brother's tomb; or academic, like Milton's
Lycidas. We are not to suppose that Milton was heart-
broken by the death of young Mr King, or that Shelley
was greatly desolated by the death of Keats, with whom
his personal relations had been slight, and of whose
poetry he had spoken evil. He was nobly stirred as
a poet by a poet's death—like Mr Swinburne by the
death of Charles Baudelaire; but neither Shelley nor
Mr Swinburne was lamenting *dimidium animæ suæ*, or
mourning for a friend

> " Dear as the mother to the son,
> More than my brothers are to me."

The passion of *In Memoriam* is personal, is acute, is
life-long, and thus it differs from the other elegies.
Moreover, it celebrates a noble object, and thus is
unlike the ambiguous affection, real or dramatic, which
informs the sonnets of Shakespeare. So the poem
stands alone, cloistered; not fiery with indignation, not
breaking into actual prophecy, like Shelley's *Adonais;*
not capable, by reason even of its meditative metre,
of the organ music of *Lycidas.* Yet it is not to be
reckoned inferior to these because its aim and plan are
other than theirs.

It is far from my purpose to "class" Tennyson, or
to dispute about his relative greatness when compared
with Wordsworth or Byron, Coleridge, Shelley, or Burns.
He rated one song of Lovelace above all his lyrics, and,

in fact, could no more have written the Cavalier's *To Althea from Prison* than Lovelace could have written the *Morte d'Arthur*. "It is not reasonable, it is not fair," says Mr Harrison, after comparing *In Memoriam* with *Lycidas*, "to compare Tennyson with Milton," and it is not reasonable to compare Tennyson with any poet whatever. Criticism is not the construction of a class list. But we may reasonably say that *In Memoriam* is a noble poem, an original poem, a poem which stands alone in literature. The wonderful beauty, ever fresh, howsoever often read, of many stanzas, is not denied by any critic. The marvel is that the same serene certainty of art broods over even the stanzas which must have been conceived while the sorrow was fresh. The second piece,

"Old yew, which graspest at the stones,"

must have been composed soon after the stroke fell. Yet it is as perfect as the proem of 1849. As a rule, the poetical expression of strong emotion appears usually to clothe the memory of passion when it has been softened by time. But here already "the rhythm, phrasing, and articulation are entirely faultless, exquisitely clear, melodious, and rare."[1] It were superfluous labour to point at special beauties, at the exquisite rendering of nature; and copious commentaries exist to explain the course of the argument, if a series of moods is to be called an argument. One may note such a

[1] Mr Harrison, *Tennyson, Ruskin, and Mill*, p. 5.

point as that (xiv.) where the poet says that, were he to
meet his friend in life,

" I should not feel it to be strange."

It may have happened to many to mistake, for a section
of a second, the face of a stranger for the face seen only
in dreams, and to find that the recognition brings no
surprise.

Pieces of a character apart from the rest, and placed
in a designed sequence, are xcii., xciii., xcv. In the
first the poet says—

" If any vision should reveal
    Thy likeness, I might count it vain
    As but the canker of the brain ;
Yea, tho' it spake and made appeal

To chances where our lots were cast
    Together in the days behind,
    I might but say, I hear a wind
Of memory murmuring the past.

Yea, tho' it spake and bared to view
    A fact within the coming year ;
    And tho' the months, revolving near,
Should prove the phantom-warning true,

They might not seem thy prophecies,
    But spiritual presentiments,
    And such refraction of events
As often rises ere they rise."

The author thus shows himself *difficile* as to recognising the personal identity of a phantasm ; nor is it easy
to see what mode of proving his identity would be left

to a spirit.   The poet, therefore, appeals to some perhaps less satisfactory experience :—

> "Descend, and touch, and enter; hear
>   The wish too strong for words to name;
>   That in this blindness of the frame
> My Ghost may feel that thine is near."

The third poem is the crown of *In Memoriam*, expressing almost such things as are not given to man to
utter :—

> And all at once it seem'd at last
> The living soul was flash'd on mine,
>
> And mine in this was wound, and whirl'd
>   About empyreal heights of thought,
>   And came on that which is, and caught
> The deep pulsations of the world,
>
> Æonian music measuring out
>   The steps of Time—the shocks of Chance—
>   The blows of Death.   At length my trance
> Was cancell'd, stricken thro' with doubt.
>
> Vague words ! but ah, how hard to frame
>   In matter-moulded forms of speech,
>   Or ev'n for intellect to reach
> Thro' memory that which I became."

Experiences like this, subjective, and not matter for
argument, were familiar to Tennyson.   Jowett said,
"He was one of those who, though not an upholder
of miracles, thought that the wonders of Heaven and
Earth were never far absent from us."   In *The Mystic*,
Tennyson, when almost a boy, had shown familiarity

with strange psychological and psychical conditions.
Poems of much later life also deal with these, and,
more or less consciously, his philosophy was tinged,
and his confidence that we are more than "cunning
casts in clay" was increased, by phenomena of experience, which can only be evidence for the mystic himself, if even for him. But this dim aspect of his philosophy, of course, is "to the Greeks foolishness."

His was a philosophy of his own ; not a philosophy
for disciples, and "those that eddy round and round."
It was the sum of his reflection on the mass of his
impressions. I have shown, by the aid of dates, that
it was not borrowed from Huxley, Mr Stopford
Brooke, or the late Duke of Argyll. But, no doubt,
many of the ideas were "in the air," and must have
presented themselves to minds at once of religious
tendency, and attracted by the evolutionary theories
which had always existed as floating speculations, till
they were made current coin by the genius and patient
study of Darwin. That Tennyson's opinions between
1830 and 1840 were influenced by those of F. D.
Maurice is reckoned probable by Canon Ainger, author
of the notice of the poet in *The Dictionary of National
Biography*. In the Life of Maurice, Tennyson does
not appear till 1850, and the two men were not at
Cambridge together. But Maurice's ideas, as they
then existed, may have reached Tennyson orally
through Hallam and other members of the Trinity
set, who knew personally the author of *Letters to a*

Quaker. However, this is no question of scientific priority : to myself it seems that Tennyson "beat his music out" for himself, as perhaps most people do. Like his own Sir Percivale, "I know not all he meant."

Among the opinions as to *In Memoriam* current at the time of its publication Lord Tennyson notices those of Maurice and Robertson. They "thought that the poet had made a definite step towards the unification of the highest religion and philosophy with the progressive science of the day." Neither science nor religion stands still; neither stands now where it then did. Conceivably they are travelling on paths which will ultimately coincide; but this opinion, of course, must seem foolishness to most professors of science. Bishop Westcott was at Cambridge when the book appeared : he is one of Mr Harrison's possible sources of Tennyson's ideas. He recognised the poet's "splendid faith (in the face of every difficulty) in the growing purpose of the sum of life, and in the noble destiny of the individual man." Ten years later Professor Henry Sidgwick, a mind sufficiently sceptical, found in some lines of *In Memoriam* "the indestructible and inalienable minimum of faith which humanity cannot give up because it is necessary for life; and which I know that I, at least so far as the man in me is deeper than the methodical thinker, cannot give up." But we know that many persons not only do not find an irreducible minimum of faith "necessary for life," but are highly indignant and contemptuous if any one else ventures to suggest the logical possibility of any faith at all.

The mass of mankind will probably never be convinced unbelievers—nay, probably the backward or forward swing of the pendulum will touch more convinced belief. But there always have been, since the *Rishis* of India sang, superior persons who believe in nothing not material—whatever the material may be. Tennyson was, it is said, "impatient" of these *esprits forts*, and they are impatient of him. It is an error to be impatient: we know not whither the *logos* may lead us, or later generations; and we ought not to be irritated with others because it leads them into what we think the wrong path. It is unfortunate that a work of art, like *In Memoriam*, should arouse theological or anti-theological passions. The poet only shows us the paths by which his mind travelled: they may not be the right paths, nor is it easy to trace them on a philosophical chart. He escaped from Doubting Castle. Others may "take that for a hermitage," and be happy enough in the residence. We are all determined by our bias: Tennyson's is unconcealed. His poem is not a tract: it does not aim at the conversion of people with the contrary bias. It is irksome, in writing about a poet, to be obliged to discuss a philosophy which, certainly, is not stated in the manner of Spinoza, but is merely the equilibrium of contending forces in a single mind.

The most famous review of *In Memoriam* is that

which declared that "these touching lines evidently
come from the full heart of the widow of a military
man." This is only equalled, if equalled, by a recent
critique which treated a fresh edition of *Jane Eyre* as a
new novel, "not without power, in parts, and showing
some knowledge of Yorkshire local colour."

VI.

On June 13 Tennyson married, at Shiplake, the object of his old, long-tried, and constant affection.   The marriage was still "imprudent,"—eight years of then uncontested supremacy in English poetry had not brought a golden harvest.   Mr Moxon appears to have supplied £300 "in advance of royalties."   The sum, so contemptible in the eyes of first-rate modern novelists, was a competence to Tennyson, added to his little pension and the *épaves* of his patrimony.   "The peace of God came into my life when I married her," he said in later days.   The poet made a charming copy of verses to his friend, the Rev. Mr Rawnsley, who tied the knot, as he and his bride drove to the beautiful village of Pangbourne.   Thence they went to the stately Clevedon Court, the seat of Sir Abraham Elton, hard by the church where Arthur Hallam sleeps.   The place is very ancient and beautiful, and was a favourite haunt of Thackeray.   They passed on to Lynton, and to Glastonbury, where a collateral ancestor of Mrs Tennyson's is

buried beside King Arthur's grave, in that green valley of
Avilion, among the apple-blossoms.   They settled for a
while at Tent Lodge on Coniston Water, in a land of
hospitable Marshalls.

After their return to London, on the night of
November 18, Tennyson dreamed that Prince Albert
came and kissed him, and that he himself said,
" Very kind, but very German," which was very like
him.   Next day he received from Windsor the offer of
the Laureateship.   He doubted, and hesitated, but
accepted.   Since Wordsworth's death there had, as
usual, been a good deal of banter about the probable
new Laureate : examples of competitive odes exist in
Bon Gaultier.   That by Tennyson is Anacreontic, but
he was not really set on kissing the Maids of Honour,
as he is made to sing.   Rogers had declined, on the
plea of extreme old age ; but it was worthy of the great
and good Queen not to overlook the Nestor of English
poets.   For the rest, the Queen looked for " a name
bearing such distinction in the literary world as to do
credit to the appointment."   In the previous century
the great poets had rarely been Laureates.   But since
Sir Walter Scott declined the bays in favour of Southey,
for whom, again, the tale of bricks in the way of Odes
was lightened, and when Wordsworth succeeded Southey,
the office became honourable.   Tennyson gave it an
increase of renown, while, though in itself of merely
nominal value, it served his poems, to speak profanely,
as an advertisement   New editions of his books were

at once in demand ; while few readers had ever heard of
Mr Browning, already his friend, and already author of
Men and Women.

The Laureateship brought the poet acquainted with
the Queen, who was to be his debtor in later days for
encouragement and consolation. To his Laureateship
we owe, among other good things, the stately and
moving *Ode on the Death of the Duke of Wellington*,
a splendid heroic piece, unappreciated at the moment.
But Tennyson was, of course, no Birthday poet. Since
the exile of the House of Stuart our kings in England
have not maintained the old familiarity with many
classes of their subjects. Literature has not been
fashionable at Court, and Tennyson could in no age
have been a courtier. We hear the complaint, every
now and then, that official honours are not conferred
(except the Laureateship) on men of letters. But most
of them probably think it rather distinguished not to be
decorated, or to carry titles borne by many deserving
persons unvisited by the Muses. Even the appointment
to the bays usually provokes a great deal of jealous and
spiteful feeling, which would only be multiplied if official
honours were distributed among men of the pen. Perhaps Tennyson's laurels were not for nothing in the
chorus of dispraise which greeted the *Ode on the Duke
of Wellington*, and *Maud*.

The year 1851 was chiefly notable for a tour to Italy,
made immortal in the beautiful poem of *The Daisy*,
in a measure of the poet's own invention. The next

year, following on the *Coup d'état* and the rise of the
new French empire, produced patriotic appeals to
Britons to " guard their own," which to a great extent
former alien owners had been unsuccessful in guarding
from Britons.   The Tennysons had lost their first child
at his birth : perhaps he is remembered in *The Grandmother*, " the babe had fought for his life."   In August
1852 the present Lord Tennyson was born, and Mr
Maurice was asked to be godfather.   The Wellington
Ode was of November, and was met by " the almost
universal depreciation of the press,"—why, except because, as I have just suggested, Tennyson was Laureate,
it is impossible to imagine.   The verses were worthy of
the occasion : more they could not be.

In the autumn of 1853 the poet visited Ardtornish
on the Sound of Mull, a beautiful place endeared
to him who now writes by the earliest associations.
It chanced to him to pass his holidays there just
when Tennyson and Mr Palgrave had left — " Mr
Tinsmith and Mr Pancake," as Robert the boatman,
a very black Celt, called them.   Being then nine
years of age, I heard of a poet's visit, and asked, " A
real poet, like Sir Walter Scott ? " with whom I then
supposed that " the Muse had gone away."   " Oh,
not like Sir Walter Scott, of course," my mother told
me, with loyalty unashamed.   One can think of the
poet as Mrs Sellar, his hostess, describes him, beneath
the limes of the avenue at Acharn, planted, Mrs Sellar
says, by a cousin of Flora Macdonald.   I have been

told that the lady who planted the lilies, if not the limes, was the famed Jacobite, Miss Jennie Cameron, mentioned in *Tom Jones.* An English engraving of 1746 shows the Prince between these two beauties, Flora and Jennie.

"No one," says Mrs Sellar, "could have been more easy, simple, and delightful," and indeed it is no marvel that in her society and that of her husband, the Greek professor, and her cousin, Miss Cross, and in such scenes, "he blossomed out in the most genial manner, making us all feel as if he were an old friend."

In November Tennyson took a house at Farringford, "as it was beautiful and far from the haunts of men." There he settled to a country existence in the society of his wife, his two children (the second, Lionel, being in 1854 the baby), and there he composed *Maud,* while the sound of the guns, in practice for the war of the Crimea, boomed from the coast. In May Tennyson saw the artists, of schools oddly various, who illustrated his poems. Millais, Rossetti, and Holman Hunt gave the tone to the art, but Mr Horsley, Creswick, and Mulgrave were also engaged. While *Maud* was being composed Tennyson wrote *The Charge of the Light Brigade ;* a famous poem, not in a manner in which he was born to excel—at least in my poor opinion. "Some one *had* blundered," and that line was the first fashioned and the keynote of the poem ; but, after all, "blundered" is not an exquisite rhyme to "hundred." The poem, in any case, was most welcome to our army in the Crimea, and is a spirited piece for recitation.

In January 1855 *Maud* was finished; in April the poet copied it out for the press, and refreshed himself by reading a very different poem, *The Lady of the Lake*. The author, Sir Walter, had suffered, like the hero of *Maud*, by an unhappy love affair, which just faintly colours *The Lady of the Lake* by a single allusion, in the description of Fitz-James's dreams :—

> "Then,—from my couch may heavenly might
> Chase that worst phantom of the night !—
> Again returned the scenes of youth,
> Of confident undoubting truth ;
> Again his soul he interchanged
> With friends whose hearts were long estranged.
> They come, in dim procession led,
> The cold, the faithless, and the dead ;
> As warm each hand, each brow as gay,
> As if they parted yesterday.
> And doubt distracts him at the view—
> Oh, were his senses false or true ?
> Dreamed he of death, or broken vow,
> Or is it all a vision now ? "

We learn from Lady Louisa Stuart, to whom Scott read these lines, that they referred to his lost love. I cite the passage because the extreme reticence of Scott, in his undying sorrow, is in contrast with what Tennyson, after reading *The Lady of the Lake*, was putting into the mouth of his complaining lover in *Maud*.

We have no reason to suppose that Tennyson himself had ever to bewail a faithless love. To be sure, the hero of *Locksley Hall* is in this attitude, but then *Locksley Hall* is not autobiographical. Less dramatic and impersonal in appearance are the stanzas—

> "Come not, when I am dead,
> To drop thy foolish tears upon my grave;"

and

> "Child, if it were thine error or thy crime
> I care no longer, being all unblest."

No biographer tells us whether this was a personal complaint or a mere set of verses on an imaginary occasion. In *In Memoriam* Tennyson speaks out concerning the loss of a friend. In *Maud*, as in *Locksley Hall*, he makes his hero reveal the agony caused by the loss of a mistress. There is no reason to suppose that the poet had ever any such mischance, but many readers have taken *Locksley Hall* and *Maud* for autobiographical revelations, like *In Memoriam*. They are, on the other hand, imaginative and dramatic. They illustrate the pangs of disappointed love of woman, pangs more complex and more rankling than those inflicted by death. In each case, however, the poet, who has sung so nobly the happiness of fortunate wedded loves, has chosen a hero with whom we do not readily sympathise—a Hamlet in miniature,

> "With a heart of furious fancies,"

as in the old mad song. This choice, thanks to the popular misconception, did him some harm. As a "monodramatic Idyll," a romance in many rich lyric

measures, *Maud* was at first excessively unpopular.
"Tennyson's *Maud* is Tennyson's Maudlin," said a
satirist, and "morbid," "mad," "rampant," and "rabid
bloodthirstiness of soul," were among the amenities of
criticism. Tennyson hated war, but his hero, at least,
hopes that national union in a national struggle will
awake a nobler than the commercial spirit. Into the
rights and wrongs of our quarrel with Russia we are not
to go. Tennyson, rightly or wrongly, took the part of
his country, and must "thole the feud" of those high-
souled citizens who think their country always in the
wrong—as perhaps it very frequently is. We are not to
expect a tranquil absence of bias in the midst of
military excitement, when very laudable sentiments are
apt to misguide men in both directions. In any case,
political partisanship added to the enemies of the
poem, which was applauded by Henry Taylor, Ruskin,
George Brimley, and Jowett, while Mrs Browning sent
consoling words from Italy. The poem remained a
favourite with the author, who chose passages from it
often, when persuaded to read aloud by friends ; and
modern criticism has not failed to applaud the splendour
of the verse and the subtlety of the mad scenes, the
passion of the love lyrics.

These merits have ceased to be disputed, but, though
a loyal Tennysonian, I have never quite been able to
reconcile myself to *Maud* as a whole. The hero is an
unwholesome young man, and not of an original kind.
He is *un beau ténébreux* of 1830. I suppose it has been

observed that he is merely The Master of Ravenswood in modern costume, and without Lady Ashton. Her part is taken by Maud's brother. The situations of the hero and of the Master (whose acquaintance Thackeray never renewed after he lost his hat in the Kelpie Flow) are nearly identical. The families and fathers of both have been ruined by "the gray old wolf," and by Sir William Ashton, representing the house of Stair. Both heroes live dawdling on, hard by their lost ancestral homes. Both fall in love with the daughters of the enemies of their houses. The loves of both are baffled, and end in tragedy. Both are concerned in a duel, though the Master, on his way to the ground, "stables his steed in the Kelpie Flow," and the wooer in *Maud* shoots Lucy Ashton's brother,—I mean the brother of Maud,—though duelling in England was out of date. Then comes an interval of madness, and he recovers amid the patriotic emotions of the ill-fated Crimean expedition. Both lovers are gloomy, though the Master has better cause, for the Tennysonian hero is more comfortably provided for than Edgar with his "man and maid," his Caleb and Mysie. Finally, both *The Bride of Lammermoor*, which affected Tennyson so potently in boyhood

("*A merry merry bridal,*
A merry merry day"),

and *Maud*, excel in passages rather than as wholes.

The hero of *Maud*, with his clandestine wooing of a

girl of sixteen, has this apology, that the match had
been, as it were, predestined, and desired by the mother
of the lady.   Still, the brother did not ill to be angry ;
and the peevishness of the hero against the brother and
the parvenu lord and rival strikes a jarring note.   In
England, at least, the general sentiment is opposed to
this moody, introspective kind of young man, of whom
Tennyson is not to be supposed to approve.   We do
not feel certain that his man and maid were "ever ready
to slander and steal."   That seems to be part of his
jaundiced way of looking at everything and everybody.
He has even a bad word for the " man-god " of
modern days,—

"The man of science himself is fonder of glory, and vain,
    An eye well-practised in nature, a spirit bounded and
        poor."

Rien n'est sacré for this cynic, who thinks himself a
Stoic.   Thus *Maud* was made to be unpopular with the
author's countrymen, who conceived a prejudice against
Maud's lover, described by Tennyson as "a morbid
poetic soul, . . . an egotist with the makings of a
cynic."   That he is "raised to sanity" (still in Tennyson's words) " by a pure and holy love which elevates
his whole nature," the world failed to perceive, especially
as the sanity was only a brief lucid interval, tempered
by hanging about the garden to meet a girl of sixteen,
unknown to her relations.   Tennyson added that " different phases of passion in one person take the place of

different characters," to which critics replied that they wanted different characters, if only by way of relief, and did not care for any of the phases of passion. The learned Monsieur Janet has maintained that love is a disease like another, and that nobody falls in love when in perfect health of mind and body. This theory seems open to exception, but the hero of Maud is unhealthy enough. At best and last, he only helps to give a martial force a "send-off":—

> " I stood on a giant deck and mixed my breath
> With a loyal people shouting a battle-cry."

He did not go out as a volunteer, and probably the Crimean winters brought him back to his original estate of cynical gloom—and very naturally.

The reconciliation with Life is not like the reconciliation of *In Memoriam.* The poem took its rise in old lines, and most beautiful lines, which Tennyson had contributed in 1837 to a miscellany :—

> " O that 'twere possible,
>> After long grief and pain,
>> To find the arms of my true love
>> Round me once again."

Thence the poet, working back to find the origin of the situation, encountered the ideas and the persons of *Maud.*

I have tried to state the sources, in the general mind, of the general dislike of *Maud.* The public, "driving at practice," disapproved of the " criticism of

life" in the poem ; confused the suffering narrator with
the author, and neglected the poetry. "No modern
poem," said Jowett, "contains more lines that ring
in the ears of men. I do not know any verse out of
Shakespeare in which the ecstacy of love soars to such
a height." With these comments we may agree, yet
may fail to follow Jowett when he says, "No poem
since Shakespeare seems to show equal power of the
same kind, or equal knowledge of human nature."
Shakespeare could not in a narrative poem have preferred the varying passions of one character to the
characters of many persons.

Tennyson was "nettled at first," his son says, "by
these captious remarks of the 'indolent reviewers,' but
afterwards he would take no notice of them except to
speak of them in a half - pitiful, half - humorous, half-
mournful manner." The besetting sin and error of the
critics was, of course, to confound Tennyson's hero with
himself, as if we confused Dickens with Pip.

Like *Aurora Leigh*, *Lucile*, and other works, *Maud*
is under the disadvantage of being, practically, a novel of
modern life in verse. Criticised as a tale of modern life
(and it was criticised in that character), it could not be
very highly esteemed. But the essence of *Maud*, of
course, lies in the poetical vehicle. Nobody can cavil
at the impressiveness of the opening stanzas—

" I hate the dreadful hollow behind the little wood " ;

with the keynotes of colour and of desolation struck ;

the lips of the hollow "dabbled with blood-red heath,"
the "red-ribb'd ledges," and "the flying gold of the
ruin'd woodlands"; and the contrast in the picture of
the child Maud—

"Maud the delight of the village, the ringing joy of the Hall."

The poem abounds in lines which live in the memory,
as in the vernal description—

" A million emeralds break from the ruby-budded lime ";

and the voice heard in the garden singing

"A passionate ballad gallant and gay,"

as Lovelace's *Althea ;* and the lines on the far-off waving
of a white hand, "betwixt the cloud and the moon."
The lyric of

> " Birds in the high Hall-garden
> When twilight was falling,
> Maud, Maud, Maud, Maud,
> They were crying and calling,"

was a favourite of the poet.

" What birds were these ? " he is said to have asked
a lady suddenly, when reading to a silent company.

" Nightingales," suggested a listener, who did not
probably remember any other fowl that is vocal in the
dusk.

" No, they were rooks," answered the poet.

" Come into the Garden, Maud," is as fine a love-
song as Tennyson ever wrote, with a triumphant ring,
and a soaring exultant note.   Then the poem drops

from its height, like a lark shot high in heaven ; tragedy comes, and remorse, and the beautiful interlude
of the

"lovely shell,
Small and pure as a pearl."

Then follows the exquisite

"O that 'twere possible,"

and the dull consciousness of the poem of madness,
with its dumb gnawing confusion of pain and wandering
memory ; the hero being finally left, in the author's
words, "sane but shattered."

Tennyson's letters of the time show that the critics
succeeded in wounding him : it was not a difficult thing
to do. *Maud* was threatened with a broadside from "that
pompholygous, broad - blown Apollodorus, the gifted
X." People who have read Aytoun's diverting *Firmilian*,
where Apollodorus plays his part, and who remember
"gifted Gilfillan" in *Waverley*, know who the gifted X.
was. But X. was no great authority south of Tay.

Despite the almost unanimous condemnation by
public critics, the success of *Maud* enabled Tennyson
to buy Farringford, so he must have been better
appreciated and understood by the world than by the
reviewers.

In February 1850 Tennyson returned to his old
Arthurian themes, "the only big thing not done," for
Milton had merely glanced at Arthur, Dryden did not

"Raise the Table Round again,"

and Blackmore has never been reckoned adequate.
Vivien was first composed as *Merlin and Nimue,* and
then *Geraint and Enid* was adapted from the *Mabinogion,* the Welsh collection of *Märchen* and legends,
things of widely different ages, now rather Celtic, or
Brythonic, now amplifications made under the influence
of mediæval French romance. *Enid* was finished in
Wales in August, and Tennyson learned Welsh enough
to be able to read the *Mabinogion,* which is much more
of Welsh than many Arthurian critics possess. The two
first Idylls were privately printed in the summer of 1857,
being very rare and much desired of collectors in this
embryonic shape. In July *Guinevere* was begun, in the
middle, with Arthur's valedictory address to his erring
consort. In autumn Tennyson visited the late Duke of
Argyll at Inveraray : he was much attached to the Duke
—unlike Professor Huxley. Their love of nature, the
Duke being as keen-eyed as the poet was short-sighted,
was one tie of union. The Indian Mutiny, or at least
the death of Havelock, was the occasion of lines which
the author was too wise to include in any of his volumes :
the poem on Lucknow was of later composition.

Guinevere was completed in March 1858; and
Tennyson met Mr Swinburne, then very young. "What
I particularly admired in him was that he did not press
upon me any verses of his own." Tennyson would have
found more to admire if he had pressed for a sight of
the verses. Neither he nor Mr Matthew Arnold was
very encouraging to young poets : they had no sons in

Apollo, like Ben Jonson. But both were kept in a perpetual state of apprehension by the army of versifiers who send volumes by post, to whom that can only be said what Tennyson did say to one of them, "As an amusement to yourself and your friends, the writing it" (verse) "is all very well." It is the friends who do not find it amusing, while the stranger becomes the foe. The psychology of these pests of the Muses is bewildering. They do not seem to read poetry, only to write it and launch it at unoffending strangers. If they bought each other's books, all of them could afford to publish.

The Master of Balliol, the most adviceful man, if one may use the term, of his age, appears to have advised Tennyson to publish the *Idylls* at once. There had been years of silence since *Maud*, and the Master suspected that "mosquitoes" (reviewers) were the cause. "There is a note needed to show the good side of human nature and to condone its frailties which Thackeray will never strike." To others it seems that Thackeray was eternally striking this note : at that time in General Lambert, his wife, and daughters, not to speak of other characters in *The Virginians*. Who does not condone the frailties of Captain Costigan, and F. B., and the Chevalier Strong? In any case, Tennyson took his own time, he was (1858) only beginning *Elaine*. There is no doubt that Tennyson was easily pricked by unsympathetic criticism, even from the most insignificant source, and, as he confessed, he received little pleasure from praise. All authors, without exception, are sensitive. A sturdier author wrote that he would sometimes have been glad to meet his assailant "where the muir-cock was bailie." We know how testily Wordsworth replied in defence to the gentlest comments by Lamb.

The Master of Balliol kept insisting, "As to the critics, their power is not really great. . . . One drop of natural feeling in poetry or the true statement of a single new fact is already felt to be of more value than all the critics put together." Yet even critics may be in the right, and of all great poets, Tennyson listened most obediently to their censures, as we have seen in the case of his early poems. His prolonged silences after the attacks of 1833 and 1855 were occupied in work and reflection : Achilles was not merely sulking in his tent, as some of his friends seem to have supposed. An epic in a series of epic idylls cannot be dashed off like a romantic novel in rhyme ; and Tennyson's method was always one of waiting for maturity of conception and execution.

Mrs Tennyson, doubtless by her lord's desire, asked the Master (then tutor of Balliol) to suggest themes. Old age was suggested, and is treated in *The Grandmother.* Other topics were not handled. " I hold most strongly," said the Master, "that it is the duty of every one who has the good fortune to know a man of genius to do any trifling service they can to lighten his work." To do every service in his power to every man was the Master's life-long practice. He was much

G

at home, his letters show, with Burns; he especially cites *John Anderson, my jo, John*, but he tells an anecdote of Burns composing *Tam o' Shanter* with emotional tears, which, if true at all, is true of the making of *To Mary in Heaven*. If Burns wept over *Tam o' Shanter*, the tears must have been tears of laughter.

The first four *Idylls of the King* were prepared for publication in the spring of 1859; while Tennyson was at work also on *Pelleas and Ettarre*, and the Tristram cycle. In autumn he went on a tour to Lisbon with Mr F. T. Palgrave and Mr Craufurd Grove. Returning, he fell eagerly to reading an early copy of Darwin's *Origin of Species*, the crown of his own early speculations on the theory of evolution. "Your theory does not make against Christianity?" he asked Darwin later (1868), who replied, "No, certainly not." But Darwin has stated the waverings of his own mind in contact with a topic too high for *a priori* reasoning, and only to be approached, if at all, on the strength of the scientific method applied to facts which science, so far, neglects, or denies, or "explains away," rather than explains.

The *Idylls*, unlike *Maud*, were well received by the press, better by the public, and best of all by friends like Thackeray, the Duke of Argyll, the Master of Balliol, and Clough, while Ruskin showed some reserve. The letter from Thackeray I cannot deny myself the pleasure of citing from the Biography: it was written

" in an ardour of claret and gratitude," but posted some
six weeks later :—

FOLKESTONE, *September*.
36 ONSLOW SQUARE, *October*.

MY DEAR OLD ALFRED,—I owe you a letter of happiness
and thanks. Sir, about three weeks ago, when I was ill in
bed, I read the *Idylls of the King*, and I thought, " Oh, I
must write to him now, for this pleasure, this delight, this
splendour of happiness which I have been enjoying." But
I should have blotted the sheets, 'tis ill writing on one's back.
The letter full of gratitude never went as far as the post-
office, and how comes it now ?

D'abord, a bottle of claret. (The landlord of the hotel
asked me down to the cellar and treated me.)   Then afterwards sitting here, an old magazine, *Fraser's Magazine*,
1850, and I come on a poem out of *The Princess* which says,
" I hear the horns of Elfland blowing, blowing,"—no, it's " the
horns of Elfland faintly blowing " (I have been into my bed-
room to fetch my pen and it has made that blot), and, reading the lines, which only one man in the world could write,
I thought about the other horns of Elfland blowing in full
strength, and Arthur in gold armour, and Guinevere in gold
hair, and all those knights and heroes and beauties and
purple landscapes and misty gray lakes in which you have
made me live. They seem like facts to me, since about
three weeks ago (three weeks or a month was it ?) when I
read the book. It is on the table yonder, and I don't like,
somehow, to disturb it, but the delight and gratitude ! You
have made me as happy as I was as a child with the
Arabian Nights,—every step I have walked in Elfland has
been a sort of Paradise to me. (The landlord gave *two*
bottles of his claret and I think I drank the most) and here
I have been lying back in the chair and thinking of those
delightful Idylls, my thoughts being turned to you : what
could I do but be grateful to that surprising genius which
has made me so happy ? Do you understand that what I

mean is all true, and that I should break out were you sitting opposite with a pipe in your mouth? Gold and purple and diamonds, I say, gentlemen, and glory and love and honour, and if you haven't given me all these why should I be in such an ardour of gratitude? But I have had out of that dear book the greatest delight that has ever come to me since I was a young man; to write and think about it makes me almost young, and this I suppose is what I'm doing, like an after-dinner speech.

P.S.—I thought the "Grandmother" quite as fine. How can you at 50 be doing things as well as at 35?

October 16th.—(I should think six weeks after the writing of the above.)

The rhapsody of gratitude was never sent, and for a peculiar reason : just about the time of writing I came to an arrangement with Smith & Elder to edit their new magazine, and to have a contribution from T. was the publishers' and editor's highest ambition. But to ask a man for a favour, and to praise and bow down before him in the same page, seemed to be so like hypocrisy, that I held my hand, and left this note in my desk, where it has been lying during a little French-Italian-Swiss tour which my girls and their papa have been making.

Meanwhile S. E. & Co. have been making their own proposals to you, and you have replied not favourably, I am sorry to hear; but now there is no reason why you should not have my homages, and I am just as thankful for the Idylls, and love and admire them just as much, as I did two months ago when I began to write in that ardour of claret and gratitude. If you can't write for us you can't. If you can by chance some day, and help an old friend, how pleased and happy I shall be! This however must be left to fate and your convenience : I don't intend to give up hope, but accept the good fortune if it comes. I see one, two, three quarterlies advertised to-day, as all bringing laurels to laureatus. He will not refuse the private tribute of an old friend, will he? You don't know how pleased the girls were at Kensington t'other day to hear you quote their father's little verses, and he too I daresay was not disgusted. He sends you and yours his very best regards in this most heartfelt and artless

(note of admiration)!

Always yours, my dear Alfred,

W. M. THACKERAY.

Naturally this letter gave Tennyson more pleasure than all the converted critics with their favourable reviews. The Duke of Argyll announced the conversion of Macaulay. The Master found *Elaine* "the fairest, sweetest, purest love poem in the English language." As to the whole, " The allegory in the distance *greatly strengthens, also elevates, the meaning of the poem.*"

Ruskin, like some other critics, felt "the art and finish in these poems a little more than I like to feel it." Yet *Guinevere* and *Elaine* had been rapidly written and little corrected. I confess to the opinion that what a man does most easily is, as a rule, what he does best. We know that the "art and finish" of Shakespeare were spontaneous, and so were those of Tennyson. Perfection in art is sometimes more sudden than we think, but then "the long preparation for it, —that unseen germination, *that* is what we ignore and forget." But he wisely kept his pieces by him for a long time, restudying them with a fresh eye. The "unreality" of the subject also failed to please Ruskin, as it is a stumbling-block to others. He wanted poems on "the living present," a theme not selected by Homer, Shakespeare, Spenser, Milton, Virgil, or the Greek dramatists, except (among surviving plays) in the *Persæ* of Æschylus. The poet who can transfigure the hot present is fortunate, but most, and the greatest, have visited the cool quiet purlieus of the past.

VII.

THE IDYLLS OF THE KING.

THE Idylls may probably be best considered in their final shape : they are not an epic, but a series of heroic *idyllia* of the same genre as the heroic *idyllia* of Theocritus.   He wrote long after the natural age of national epic, the age of Homer.   He saw the later literary epic rise in the *Argonautica* of Apollonius Rhodius, a poem with many beauties, if rather an archaistic and elaborate revival as a whole.   The time for long narrative poems, Theocritus appears to have thought, was past, and he only ventured on the heroic *idyllia* of Heracles, and certain adventures of the Argo-nauts.   Tennyson, too, from the first believed that his pieces ought to be short.   Therefore, though he had a conception of his work as a whole, a conception long mused on, and sketched in various lights, he produced no epic, only a series of epic *idyllia*.   He had a spiritual conception, "an allegory in the distance," an allegory not to be insisted upon, though its presence was to be felt.   No longer, as in youth, did Tennyson intend

Merlin to symbolise "the sceptical understanding" (as if one were to "break into blank the gospel of" Herr Kant), or poor Guinevere to stand for the Blessed Reformation, or the Table Round for Liberal Institutions. Mercifully Tennyson never actually allegorised Arthur in that fashion. Later he thought of a musical masque of Arthur, and sketched a *scenario*. Finally Tennyson dropped both the allegory of Liberal principles and the musical masque in favour of the series of heroic idylls. There was only a "parabolic drift" in the intention. "There is no single fact or incident in the Idylls, however seemingly mystical, which cannot be explained without any mystery or allegory whatever." The Idylls ought to be read (and the right readers never dream of doing anything else) as romantic poems, just like Browning's *Childe Roland*, in which the wrong readers (the members of the Browning Society) sought for mystic mountains and marvels. Yet Tennyson had his own interpretation, "a dream of man coming into practical life and ruined by one sin." That was his "interpretation," or "allegory in the distance."

People may be heard objecting to the suggestion of any spiritual interpretation of the Arthur legends, and even to the existence of elementary morality among the Arthurian knights and ladies. There seems to be a notion that "bold bawdry and open manslaughter," as Roger Ascham said, are the staple of Tennyson's sources, whether in the mediæval French, the Welsh, or in Malory's compilation, chiefly from French sources.

Tennyson is accused of " Bowdlerising " these, and of introducing gentleness, courtesy, and conscience into a literature where such qualities were unknown.   I must confess myself ignorant of any early and popular, or "primitive" literature, in which human virtues, and the human conscience, do not play their part.   Those who object to Tennyson's handling of the great Arthurian cycle, on the ground that he is too refined and too moral, must either never have read or must long have forgotten even Malory's romance.   Thus we read, in a recent novel, that Lancelot was an *homme aux bonnes fortunes*, whereas Lancelot was the most loyal of lovers.

Among other critics, Mr Harrison has objected that the Arthurian world of Tennyson " is not quite an ideal world.   Therein lies the difficulty.   The scene, though not of course historic, has certain historic suggestions and characters."   It is not apparent who the historic characters are, for the real Arthur is but a historic phantasm.   " But then, in the midst of so much realism, the knights, from Arthur downwards, talk and act in ways with which we are familiar in modern ethical and psychological novels, but which are as impossible in real mediæval knights as a Bengal tiger or a Polar bear would be in a drawing-room."   I confess to little acquaintance with modern ethical novels ; but real mediæval knights, and still more the knights of mediæval romance, were capable of very ethical actions.   To halt an army for the protection and comfort of a laundress was a highly ethical

action. Perhaps Sir Redvers Buller would do it:
Bruce did. Mr Harrison accuses the ladies of the
Idylls of soul-bewildering casuistry, like that of women
in *Middlemarch* or *Helbeck of Bannisdale*. Now I am
not reminded by Guinevere, and Elaine, and Enid, of
ladies in these ethical novels. But the women of the
mediæval *Cours d'Amour* (the originals from whom the
old romancers drew) were nothing if not casuists.
"Spiritual delicacy" (as they understood it) was their
delight.

Mr Harrison even argues that Malory's men lived
hot-blooded lives in fierce times, "before an idea had
arisen in the world of 'reverencing conscience,' 'leading sweet lives,'" and so on. But he admits that they
had "fantastic ideals of 'honour' and 'love.'" As to
"fantastic," that is a matter of opinion, but to have
ideals and to live in accordance with them is to "reverence conscience," which the heroes of the romances are
said by Mr Harrison never to have had an idea of
doing. They are denied even "amiable words and
courtliness." Need one say that courtliness is the
dominant note of mediæval knights, in history as in
romance? With discourtesy Froissart would "head
the count of crimes." After a battle, he says, Scots
knights and English would thank each other for a good
fight, "not like the Germans." "And now, I dare
say," said Malory's Sir Ector, "thou, Sir Lancelot, wast
the curtiest knight that ever bare shield, . . . and thou
wast the meekest man and the gentlest that ever ate in

hall among ladies." Observe Sir Lancelot in the
difficult pass where the Lily Maid offers her love:
"Jesu defend me, for then I rewarded your father and
your brother full evil for their great goodness. . . . But
because, fair damsel, that ye love me as ye say ye do, I
will, for your good will and kindness, show you some
goodness, . . . and always while I live to be your true
knight." Here are "amiable words and courtesy." I
cannot agree with Mr Harrison that Malory's book is
merely "a fierce lusty epic." That was not the opinion
of its printer and publisher, Caxton. He produced it
as an example of "the gentle and virtuous deeds that
some knights used in these days, . . . noble and
renowned acts of humanity, gentleness, and chivalry.
For herein may be seen noble chivalry, courtesy,
humanity, friendliness, love, cowardice, murder, hate,
virtue, and sin. Do after the good and leave the evil."

In reaction against the bold-faced heroines and
sensual amours of some of the old French romances, an
ideal of exaggerated asceticism, of stainless chastity,
notoriously pervades the portion of Malory's work
which deals with the Holy Grail. Lancelot is distraught when he finds that, by dint of enchantment,
he has been made false to Guinevere (Book XI. chap.
viii.) After his dreaming vision of the Holy Grail,
with the reproachful Voice, Sir Lancelot said, "My
sin and my wickedness have brought me great dishonour, . . . and now I see and understand that
my old sin hindereth and shameth me." He was

human, the Lancelot of Malory, and "fell to his old love again," with a heavy heart, and with long penance at the end. How such good knights can be deemed conscienceless and void of courtesy one knows not, except by a survival of the Puritanism of Ascham. But Tennyson found in the book what is in the book— honour, conscience, courtesy, and the hero—

"Whose honour rooted in dishonour stood,
And faith unfaithful kept him falsely true."

Malory's book, which was Tennyson's chief source, ends by being the tragedy of the conscience of Lancelot. Arthur is dead, or "In Avalon he groweth old." The Queen and Lancelot might sing, as Lennox reports that Queen Mary did after Darnley's murder—

"Weel is me
For I am free."

"Why took they not their pastime?" Because conscience forbade, and Guinevere sends her lover far from her, and both die in religion. Thus Malory's "fierce lusty epic" is neither so lusty nor so fierce but that it gives Tennyson his keynote: the sin that breaks the fair companionship, and is bitterly repented.

"The knights are almost too polite to kill each other," the critic urges. In Malory they are sometimes quite too polite to kill each other. Sir Darras has a blood-feud against Sir Tristram, and Sir Tristram is in his dungeon. Sir Darras said, "Wit ye well that Sir Darras shall never destroy such a noble knight as thou

art in prison, howbeit that thou hast slain three of my
sons, whereby I was greatly aggrieved. But now shalt
thou go and thy fellows. . . . All that ye did," said Sir
Darras, "was by force of knighthood, and that was the
cause I would not put you to death" (Book IX.
chap. xl.)

Tennyson is accused of "emasculating the fierce lusty
epic into a moral lesson, as if it were to be performed in
a drawing-room by an academy of young ladies"—pre-
sided over, I daresay, by "Anglican clergymen." I know
not how any one who has read the *Morte d'Arthur* can
blame Tennyson in the matter. Let Malory and his
sources be blamed, if to be moral is to be culpable. A
few passages apart, there is no coarseness in Malory ;
that there are conscience, courtesy, "sweet lives,"
"keeping down the base in man," "amiable words," and
all that Tennyson gives, and, in Mr Harrison's theory,
gives without authority in the romance, my quotations
from Malory demonstrate. They are chosen at a casual
opening of his book. That there "had not arisen in
the world" "the idea of reverencing conscience" before
the close of the fifteenth century A.D. is an extraordinary
statement for a critic of history to offer.

Mr Harrison makes his protest because "in the con-
spiracy of silence into which Tennyson's just fame has
hypnotised the critics, it is bare honesty to admit defects."
I think I am not hypnotised, and I do not regard the
Idylls as the crown of Tennyson's work. But it is not
his "defect" to have introduced generosity, gentleness,

conscience, and chastity where no such things occur in his sources. Take Sir Darras: his position is that of Priam when he meets Achilles, who slew his sons, except that Priam comes as a suppliant ; Sir Darras has Tristram in his hands, and may slay him. He is "too polite," as Mr Harrison says : he is too good a Christian, or too good a gentleman. One would not have given a tripod for the life of Achilles had he fallen into the hands of Priam. But between 1200 B.C. (or so) and the date of Malory, new ideas about "living sweet lives" had arisen. Where and when do they not arise ? A British patrol fired on certain Swazis in time of truce. Their lieutenant, who had been absent when this occurred, rode alone to the stronghold of the Swazi king, Sekukoeni, and gave himself up, expecting death by torture. "Go, sir," said the king ; "we too are gentlemen." The idea of a "sweet life" of honour had dawned even on Sekukoeni : it lights up Malory's romance, and is reflected in Tennyson's Idylls, doubtless with some modernism of expression.

That the Idylls represent no real world is certain. That Tennyson modernises and moralises too much, I willingly admit ; what I deny is that he introduces gentleness, courtesy, and conscience where his sources have none. Indeed this is not a matter of critical opinion, but of verifiable fact. Any one can read Malory and judge for himself. But the world in which the Idylls move could not be real. For more than a thousand years different races, different ages, had taken

hold of the ancient Celtic legends and spiritualised them
after their own manner, and moulded them to their own
ideals.   There may have been a historical Arthur,
Comes Britanniæ, after the Roman withdrawal.   *Ye
Amherawdyr Arthur*, "the Emperor Arthur," may have
lived and fought, and led the Brythons to battle.   But
there may also have been a Brythonic deity, or culture
hero, of the same, or of a similar name, and myths about
him may have been assigned to a real Arthur.   Again,
the Arthur of the old Welsh legends was by no means
the blameless king—even in comparatively late French
romances he is not blameless.   But the process of idealising him went on : still incomplete in Malory's compilation, where he is often rather otiose and far from royal.
Tennyson, for his purpose, completed the idealisation.

As to Guinevere, she was not idealised in the old
Welsh rhyme—

> "Guinevere, Giant Ogurvan's daughter,
>   Naughty young, more naughty later."

Of Lancelot, and her passion for him, the old Welsh
has nothing to say.   Probably Chrétien de Troyes, by
a happy blunder or misconception, gave Lancelot his
love and his pre-eminent part.   Lancelot was confused
with Peredur, and Guinevere with the lady of whom
Peredur was in quest.   The Elaine who becomes by
Lancelot the mother of Galahad "was Lancelot's
rightful consort, as one recognises in her name that
of Elen, the Empress, whom the story of Peredur"

(Lancelot, by the confusion) "gives that hero to wife."
The second Elaine, the maid of Astolat, is another re-
fraction from the original Elen. As to the Grail, it
may be a Christianised rendering of one or another of
the magical and mystic caldrons of Welsh or Irish
legend. There is even an apparent Celtic source of the
mysterious fisher king of the Grail romance.[1]

A sketch of the evolution of the Arthurian legends
might run thus :—

Sixth to eighth century, growth of myth about an
Arthur, real, or supposed to be real.

Tenth century, the Duchies of Normandy and Brittany
are in close relations; by the eleventh century
Normans know Celtic Arthurian stories.

After 1066, Normans in contact with the Celtic
peoples of this island are in touch with the Arthur
tales.

1130-1145, works on Arthurian matter by Geoffrey of
Monmouth.

1155, Wace's French translation of Geoffrey.

1150-1182, Chrétien de Troyes writes poems on
Arthurian topics.

French prose romances on Arthur, from, say, 1180 to
1250. Those romances reach Wales, and modify,
in translations, the original Welsh legends, or, in
part, supplant them.

---

[1] The English reader may consult Mr Rhys's *The Arthurian
Legend*, Oxford, 1891, and Mr Nutt's *Studies of the Legend of the
Holy Grail*, which will direct him to other authorities and sources.

Amplifications and recastings are numerous. In 1485 Caxton publishes Malory's selections from French and English sources, the whole being Tennyson's main source, *Le Mort d'Arthur*.[1]

Thus the Arthur stories, originally Celtic, originally a mass of semi-pagan legend, myth, and *märchen*, have been retold and rehandled by Norman, Englishman, and Frenchman, taking on new hues, expressing new ideals —religious, chivalrous, and moral. Any poet may work his will on them, and Tennyson's will was to retain the chivalrous courtesy, generosity, love, and asceticism, while dimly or brightly veiling or illuminating them with his own ideals. After so many processes, from folk-tale to modern idyll, the Arthurian world could not be real, and real it is not. Camelot lies "out of space, out of time," though the colouring is mainly that of the later chivalry, and "the gleam" on the hues is partly derived from Celtic fancy of various dates, and is partly Tennysonian.

As the Idylls were finally arranged, the first, *The Coming of Arthur*, is a remarkable proof of Tennyson's ingenuity in construction. Tales about the birth of Arthur varied. In Malory, Uther Pendragon, the Bretwalda (in later phrase) of Britain, besieges the Duke of Tintagil, who has a fair wife, Ygerne, in another

---

[1] I have summarised, with omissions, Miss Jessie L. Weston's sketch in *King Arthur and his Knights*. Nutt, 1899. The learning of the subject is enormous; Dr Sommer's *Le Mort d'Arthur*, the second volume, may be consulted. Nutt, 1899.

castle. Merlin magically puts on Uther the shape of Ygerne's husband, and as her husband she receives him. On that night Arthur is begotten by Uther, and the Duke of Tintagil, his mother's husband, is slain in a sortie. Uther weds Ygerne; both recognise Arthur as their child. However, by the Celtic custom of fosterage the infant is intrusted to Sir Ector as his *dalt*, or foster-child, and Uther falls in battle. Arthur is later approven king by the adventure of drawing from the stone the magic sword that no other king could move. This adventure answers to Sigmund's drawing the sword from the Branstock, in the Volsunga Saga, "Now men stand up, and none would fain be the last to lay hand to the sword," apparently stricken into the pillar by Woden. "But none who came thereto might avail to pull it out, for in nowise would it come away howsoever they tugged at it, but now up comes Sigmund, King Volsung's son, and sets hand to the sword, and pulls it from the stock, even as if it lay loose before him." The incident in the Arthurian as in the Volsunga legend is on a par with the Golden Bough, in the sixth book of the *Æneid*. Only the predestined champion, such as Æneas, can pluck, or break, or cut the bough—

> "Ipse volens facilisque sequetur
> Si te fata vocant."

All this ancient popular element in the Arthur story is disregarded by Tennyson. He does not make Uther approach Ygerne in the semblance of her lord, as

Zeus approached Alcmena in the semblance of her husband, Amphitryon. He neglects the other ancient test of the proving of Arthur by his success in drawing the sword. The poet's object is to enfold the origin and birth of Arthur in a spiritual mystery. This is deftly accomplished by aid of the various versions of the tale that reach King Leodogran when Arthur seeks the hand of his daughter Guinevere, for Arthur's title to the crown is still disputed, so Leodogran makes inquiries. The answers first leave it dubious whether Arthur is son of Gorloïs, husband of Ygerne, or of Uther, who slew Gorloïs and married her :—

> "Enforced she was to wed him in her tears."

The Celtic custom of fosterage is overlooked, and Merlin gives the child to Anton, not as the customary *dalt*, but to preserve the babe from danger. Queen Bellicent then tells Leodogran, from the evidence of Bleys, Merlin's master in necromancy, the story of Arthur's miraculous advent.

> "And down the wave and in the flame was borne
> A naked babe, and rode to Merlin's feet,
> Who stoopt and caught the babe, and cried 'The King !
> Here is an heir for Uther !'"

But Merlin, when asked by Bellicent to corroborate the statement of Bleys, merely

> "Answer'd in riddling triplets of old time."

Finally, Leodogran's faith is confirmed by a vision.

Thus doubtfully, amidst rumour and portent, cloud and spiritual light, comes Arthur : "from the great deep" he comes, and in as strange fashion, at the end, "to the great deep he goes"—a king to be accepted in faith or rejected by doubt.   Arthur and his ideal are objects of belief.   All goes well while the knights hold that

> "The King will follow Christ, and we the King,
>   In whom high God hath breathed a secret thing."

In history we find the same situation in the France of 1429—

> "The King will follow Jeanne, and we the King."

While this faith held, all went well; when the king ceased to follow, the spell was broken,—the Maid was martyred.   In this sense the poet conceives the coming of Arthur, a sign to be spoken against, a test of high purposes, a belief redeeming and ennobling till faith fails, and the little rift within the lute, the love of Lancelot and Guinevere, makes discord of the music. As matter of legend, it is to be understood that Guinevere did not recognise Arthur when first he rode below her window—

> " Since he neither wore on helm or shield
>   The golden symbol of his kinglihood."

But Lancelot was sent to bring the bride—

> " And return'd
> Among the flowers, in May, with Guinevere."

Then their long love may have begun, as in the story of Tristram sent to bring Yseult to be the bride of King Mark. In Malory, however, Lancelot does not come on the scene till after Arthur's wedding and return from his conquering expedition to Rome. Then Lancelot wins renown, "wherefore Queen Guinevere had him in favour above all other knights; and in certain he loved the Queen again above all other ladies damosels of his life." Lancelot, as we have seen, is practically a French creation, adopted to illustrate the chivalrous theory of love, with its bitter fruit. Though not of the original Celtic stock of legend, Sir Lancelot makes the romance what it is, and draws down the tragedy that originally turned on the sin of Arthur himself, the sin that gave birth to the traitor Modred. But the mediæval romancers disguised that form of the story, and the process of idealising Arthur reached such heights in the middle ages that Tennyson thought himself at liberty to paint the *Flos Regum*, "the blameless King." He followed the *Brut ab Arthur.* "In short, God has not made since Adam was, the man more perfect than Arthur." This is remote from the Arthur of the oldest Celtic legends, but justifies the poet in adapting Arthur to the ideal hero of the Idylls :—

" Ideal manhood closed in real man,
   Rather than that grey king, whose name, a ghost,
   Streams like a cloud, man-shaped, from mountain-peak,
   And cleaves to cairn and cromlech still ; or him

Of Geoffrey's book, or him of Malleor's, one
Touched by the adulterous finger of a time
That hovered between war and wantonness,
And crownings and dethronements."

The poetical beauties of *The Coming of Arthur* excel those of *Gareth and Lynette*. The sons of Lot
and Bellicent seem to have been originally regarded as
the incestuous offspring of Arthur and his sister, the
wife of King Lot.   Next it was represented that Arthur
was ignorant of the relationship.   Mr Rhys supposes
that the mythical scandal (still present in Malory as a
sin of ignorance) arose from blending the Celtic Arthur
(as Culture Hero) with an older divine personage, such
as Zeus, who marries his sister Hera.   Marriages of
brother and sister are familiar in the Egyptian royal
house, and that of the Incas.   But the poet has a
perfect right to disregard a scandalous myth which, obviously crystallised later about the figure of the mythical
Celtic Arthur, was an incongruous accretion to his
legend.   Gareth, therefore, is merely Arthur's nephew,
not son, in the poem, as are Gawain and the traitor
Modred.   The story seems to be rather mediæval
French than Celtic—a mingling of the spirit of *fabliau*
and popular fairy tale.   The poet has added to its
lightness, almost frivolity, the description of the unreal
city of Camelot, built to music, as when

"Ilion, like a mist, rose into towers."

He has also brought in the allegory of Death, which,

when faced, proves to be "a blooming boy" behind
the mask. The courtesy and prowess of Lancelot lead
up to the later development of his character.

In *The Marriage of Geraint*, a rumour has already
risen about Lancelot and the Queen, darkening the
Court, and presaging

"The world's loud whisper breaking into storm."

For this reason Geraint removes Enid from Camelot to
his own land—the poet thus early leading up to the sin
and the doom of Lancelot. But this motive does not
occur in the Welsh story of Enid and Geraint, which
Tennyson has otherwise followed with unwonted close-
ness. The tale occurs in French romances in various
forms, but it appears to have returned, by way of France
and coloured with French influences, to Wales, where it
is one of the later Mabinogion. The characters are
Celtic, and Nud, father of Edyrn, Geraint's defeated
antagonist, appears to be recognised by Mr Rhys as
"the Celtic Zeus." The manners and the tournaments
are French. In the Welsh tale Geraint and Enid are
bedded in Arthur's own chamber, which seems to be
a symbolic commutation of the *jus primæ noctis* a
custom of which the very existence is disputed. This
unseemly antiquarian detail, of course, is omitted in
the Idyll.

An abstract of the Welsh tale will show how closely
Tennyson here follows his original. News is brought
into Arthur's Court of the appearance of a white stag.

The king arranges a hunt, and Guinevere asks leave to go and watch the sport. Next morning she cannot be wakened, though the tale does not aver, like the Idyll, that she was

> "Lost in sweet dreams, and dreaming of her love
>   For Lancelot."

Guinevere wakes late, and rides through a ford of Usk to the hunt. Geraint follows, "a golden-hilted sword was at his side, and a robe and a surcoat of satin were upon him, and two shoes of leather upon his feet, and around him was a scarf of blue purple, at each corner of which was a golden apple" :—

> "But Guinevere lay late into the morn,
>   Lost in sweet dreams, and dreaming of her love
>   For Lancelot, and forgetful of the hunt ;
>   But rose at last, a single maiden with her,
>   Took horse, and forded Usk, and gain'd the wood ;
>   There, on a little knoll beside it, stay'd
>   Waiting to hear the hounds ; but heard instead
>   A sudden sound of hoofs, for Prince Geraint,
>   Late also, wearing neither hunting-dress
>   Nor weapon, save a golden-hilted brand,
>   Came quickly flashing thro' the shallow ford
>   Behind them, and so gallop'd up the knoll.
>   A purple scarf, at either end whereof
>   There swung an apple of the purest gold,
>   Sway'd round about him, as he gallop'd up
>   To join them, glancing like a dragon-fly
>   In summer suit and silks of holiday."

The encounter with the dwarf, the lady, and the knight

follows. The prose of the Mabinogi may be compared with the verse of Tennyson :—

"Geraint," said Gwenhwyvar, "knowest thou the name of that tall knight yonder?" "I know him not," said he, "and the strange armour that he wears prevents my either seeing his face or his features." "Go, maiden," said Gwenhwyvar, "and ask the dwarf who that knight is." Then the maiden went up to the dwarf; and the dwarf waited for the maiden, when he saw her coming towards him. And the maiden inquired of the dwarf who the knight was. "I will not tell thee," he answered. "Since thou art so churlish as not to tell me," said she, "I will ask him himself." "Thou shalt not ask him, by my faith," said he. "Wherefore?" said she. "Because thou art not of honour sufficient to befit thee to speak to my Lord." Then the maiden turned her horse's head towards the knight, upon which the dwarf struck her with the whip that was in his hand across the face and the eyes, until the blood flowed forth. And the maiden, through the hurt she received from the blow, returned to Gwenhwyvar, complaining of the pain. "Very rudely has the dwarf treated thee," said Geraint. "I will go myself to know who the knight is." "Go," said Gwenhwyvar. And Geraint went up to the dwarf. "Who is yonder knight?" said Geraint. "I will not tell thee," said the dwarf. "Then will I ask him himself," said he. "That wilt thou not, by my faith," said the dwarf; "thou art not honourable enough to speak with my Lord." Said Geraint, "I have spoken with men of equal rank with him." And he turned his horse's head towards the knight; but the dwarf overtook him, and struck him as he had done the maiden, so that the blood coloured the scarf that Geraint wore. Then Geraint put his hand upon the hilt of his sword, but he took counsel with himself, and considered that it would be no vengeance for him to slay the dwarf, and to be attacked unarmed by the armed knight, so he returned to where Gwenhwyvar was.

"And while they listen'd for the distant hunt,
And chiefly for the baying of Cavall,
King Arthur's hound of deepest mouth, there rode
Full slowly by a knight, lady, and dwarf;
Whereof the dwarf lagg'd latest, and the knight
Had vizor up, and show'd a youthful face,
Imperious, and of haughtiest lineaments.
And Guinevere, not mindful of his face
In the King's hall, desired his name, and sent
Her maiden to demand it of the dwarf;
Who being vicious, old and irritable,
And doubling all his master's vice of pride,
Made answer sharply that she should not know.
'Then will I ask it of himself,' she said.
'Nay, by my faith, thou shalt not,' cried the dwarf;
'Thou art not worthy ev'n to speak of him';
And when she put her horse toward the knight,
Struck at her with his whip, and she return'd
Indignant to the Queen; whereat Geraint
Exclaiming, 'Surely I will learn the name,'
Made sharply to the dwarf, and ask'd it of him,
Who answer'd as before; and when the Prince
Had put his horse in motion toward the knight,
Struck at him with his whip, and cut his cheek.
The Prince's blood spirted upon the scarf,
Dyeing it; and his quick, instinctive hand
Caught at the hilt, as to abolish him:
But he, from his exceeding manfulness,
And pure nobility of temperament,
Wroth to be wroth at such a worm, refrain'd
From ev'n a word."

The self-restraint of Geraint, who does not slay the dwarf,

> "From his exceeding manfulness
> And pure nobility of temperament,"

may appear "too polite," and too much in accord with the still undiscovered idea of "leading sweet lives." However, the uninvented idea does occur in the Welsh original : "Then Geraint put his hand upon the hilt of his sword, but he took counsel with himself, and considered that it would be no vengeance for him to slay the dwarf," while he also reflects that he would be "attacked unarmed by the armed knight." Perhaps Tennyson may be blamed for omitting this obvious motive for self-restraint. Geraint therefore follows the knight in hope of finding arms, and arrives at the town all busy with preparations for the tournament of the sparrow - hawk. This was a challenge sparrow - hawk : the knight had won it twice, and if he won it thrice it would be his to keep. The rest, in the tale, is exactly followed in the Idyll. Geraint is entertained by the ruined Yniol. The youth bears the "costrel" full of "good purchased mead" (the ruined Earl not brewing for himself), and Enid carries the manchet bread in her veil, "old, and beginning to be worn out." All Tennyson's own is the beautiful passage—

> "And while he waited in the castle court,
> The voice of Enid, Yniol's daughter, rang
> Clear thro' the open casement of the hall,
> Singing ; and as the sweet voice of a bird,
> Heard by the lander in a lonely isle,
> Moves him to think what kind of bird it is
> That sings so delicately clear, and make
> Conjecture of the plumage and the form ;
> So the sweet voice of Enid moved Geraint ;

And made him like a man abroad at morn
When first the liquid note beloved of men
Comes flying over many a windy wave
To Britain, and in April suddenly
Breaks from a coppice gemm'd with green and red,
And he suspends his converse with a friend,
Or it may be the labour of his hands,
To think or say, 'There is the nightingale';
So fared it with Geraint, who thought and said,
'Here, by God's grace, is the one voice for me.'"

Yniol frankly admits in the tale that he was in the wrong in the quarrel with his nephew. The poet, however, gives him the right, as is natural. The combat is exactly followed in the Idyll, as is Geraint's insistence in carrying his bride to Court in her faded silks. Geraint, however, leaves Court with Enid, not because of the scandal about Lancelot, but to do his duty in his own country. He becomes indolent and uxorious, and Enid deplores his weakness, and awakes his suspicions, thus :—

And one morning in the summer time they were upon their couch, and Geraint lay upon the edge of it. And Enid was without sleep in the apartment which had windows of glass. And the sun shone upon the couch. And the clothes had slipped from off his arms and his breast, and he was asleep. Then she gazed upon the marvellous beauty of his appearance, and she said, "Alas, and am I the cause that these arms and this breast have lost their glory and the war-like fame which they once so richly enjoyed !" And as she said this, the tears dropped from her eyes, and they fell upon his breast. And the tears she shed, and the words she had spoken, awoke him ; and another thing contributed to awaken him, and that was the idea that it was not in think-

ing of him that she spoke thus, but that it was because she
loved some other man more than him, and that she wished
for other society, and thereupon Geraint was troubled in his
mind, and he called his squire ; and when he came to him,
" Go quickly," said he, "and prepare my horse and my
arms, and make them ready. And do thou arise," said he
to Enid, "and apparel thyself; and cause thy horse to be
accoutred, and clothe thee in the worst riding-dress that
thou hast in thy possession. And evil betide me," said he,
"if thou returnest here until thou knowest whether I have
lost my strength so completely as thou didst say. And if it
be so, it will then be easy for thee to seek the society thou
didst wish for of him of whom thou wast thinking." So she
arose, and clothed herself in her meanest garments. " I
know nothing, Lord," said she, " of thy meaning." " Neither
wilt thou know at this time," said he.

"At last, it chanced that on a summer morn
(They sleeping each by either) the new sun
Beat thro' the blindless casement of the room,
And heated the strong warrior in his dreams ;
Who, moving, cast the coverlet aside,
And bared the knotted column of his throat,
The massive square of his heroic breast,
And arms on which the standing muscle sloped,
As slopes a wild brook o'er a little stone,
Running too vehemently to break upon it.
And Enid woke and sat beside the couch,
Admiring him, and thought within herself,
Was ever man so grandly made as he?
Then, like a shadow, past the people's talk
And accusation of uxoriousness
Across her mind, and bowing over him,
Low to her own heart piteously she said :

'O noble breast and all-puissant arms,
Am I the cause, I the poor cause that men

Reproach you, saying all your force is gone?
I *am* the cause, because I dare not speak
And tell him what I think and what they say.
And yet I hate that he should linger here ;
I cannot love my lord and not his name.
Far liefer had I gird his harness on him,
And ride with him to battle and stand by,
And watch his mightful hand striking great blows
At caitiffs and at wrongers of the world.
Far better were I laid in the dark earth,
Not hearing any more his noble voice,
Not to be folded more in these dear arms,
And darken'd from the high light in his eyes,
Than that my lord thro' me should suffer shame.
Am I so bold, and could I so stand by,
And see my dear lord wounded in the strife,
Or maybe pierced to death before mine eyes,
And yet not dare to tell him what I think,
And how men slur him, saying all his force
Is melted into mere effeminacy?
O me, I fear that I am no true wife.'

Half inwardly, half audibly she spoke,
And the strong passion in her made her weep
True tears upon his broad and naked breast,
And these awoke him, and by great mischance
He heard but fragments of her later words,
And that she fear'd she was not a true wife.
And then he thought, ' In spite of all my care,
For all my pains, poor man, for all my pains,
She is not faithful to me, and I see her
Weeping for some gay knight in Arthur's hall.'
Then tho' he loved and reverenced her too much
To dream she could be guilty of foul act,
Right thro' his manful breast darted the pang
That makes a man, in the sweet face of her
Whom he loves most, lonely and miserable.

At this he hurl'd his huge limbs out of bed,
And shook his drowsy squire awake and cried,
' My charger and her palfrey' ; then to her,
' I will ride forth into the wilderness ;
For tho' it seems my spurs are yet to win,
I have not fall'n so low as some would wish.
And thou, put on thy worst and meanest dress
And ride with me.'   And Enid ask'd, amazed,
' If Enid errs, let Enid learn her fault.'
But he, ' I charge thee, ask not, but obey.'
Then she bethought her of a faded silk,
A faded mantle and a faded veil,
And moving toward a cedarn cabinet,
Wherein she kept them folded reverently
With sprigs of summer laid between the folds,
She took them, and array'd herself therein,
Remembering when first he came on her
Drest in that dress, and how he loved her in it,
And all her foolish fears about the dress,
And all his journey to her, as himself
Had told her, and their coming to the court."

Tennyson's

"Arms on which the standing muscle sloped,
  As slopes a wild brook o'er a little stone,
  Running too vehemently to break upon it,"

is suggested perhaps by Theocritus—"The muscles on his brawny arms stood out like rounded rocks that the winter torrent 'has rolled and worn smooth, in the great swirling stream " (Idyll xxii.)

The second part of the poem follows the original less closely.   Thus Limours, in the tale, is not an old suitor of Enid ; Edyrn does not appear to the rescue ; certain cruel games, veiled in a magic mist, occur in the tale,

and are omitted by the poet ; "Gwyffert petit, so called
by the Franks, whom the Cymry call the Little King," in
the tale, is not a character in the Idyll, and, generally,
the gross Celtic exaggerations of Geraint's feats are
toned down by Tennyson.   In other respects, as when
Geraint eats the mowers' dinner, the tale supplies the
materials.   But it does not dwell tenderly on the reconciliation.   The tale is more or less in the vein of
"patient Grizel," and he who told it is more concerned
with the fighting than with *amoris redintegratio*, and the
sufferings of Enid.   The Idyll is enriched with many
beautiful pictures from nature, such as this :—

> " But at the flash and motion of the man
>   They vanish'd panic-stricken, like a shoal
>   Of darting fish, that on a summer morn
>   Adown the crystal dykes at Camelot
>   Come slipping o'er their shadows on the sand,
>   But if a man who stands upon the brink
>   But lift a shining hand against the sun,
>   There is not left the twinkle of a fin
>   Betwixt the cressy islets white in flower ;
>   So, scared but at the motion of the man,
>   Fled all the boon companions of the Earl,
>   And left him lying in the public way."

In *Balin and Balan* Tennyson displays great con-
structive power, and remarkable skill in moulding the
most recalcitrant materials.   Balin or Balyn, according
to Mr Rhys, is the Belinus of Geoffrey of Monmouth,
" whose name represents the Celtic divinity described in

Latin as Apollo Belenus or Belinus."[1] In Geoffrey,
Belinus, euhemerised, or reduced from god to hero, has
a brother, Brennius, the Celtic Brân, King of Britain
from Caithness to the Humber.   Belinus drives Brân
into exile.   " Thus it is seen that Belinus or Balyn was,
mythologically speaking, the natural enemy " (as Apollo
Belinus, the radiant god) " of the dark divinity Brân or
Balan."

If this view be correct, the two brothers answer to the
good and bad principles of myths like that of the Huron
Iouskeha the Sun, and Anatensic the Moon, or rather
Taouiscara and Iouskeha, the hostile brothers, Black
and White.[2]   These mythical brethren are, in Malory,
two knights of Northumberland, Balin the wild and
Balan.   Their adventures are mixed up with a hostile
Lady of the Lake, whom Balin slays in Arthur's presence,
with a sword which none but Balin can draw from sheath ;
and with an evil black-faced knight Garlon, invisible at
will, whom Balin slays in the castle of the knight's
brother, King Pellam.   Pursued from room to room by
Pellam, Balin finds himself in a chamber full of relics of
Joseph of Arimathea.   There he seizes a spear, the very
spear with which the Roman soldier pierced the side of
the Crucified, and wounds Pellam.   The castle falls in

---

[1] Βέλενος and Βήληνος.   He is referred to in inscriptions, *e.g.*
Berlin, *Corpus*, iii. 4774, v. 732, 733, 1829, 2143-46 ; xii. 401.   See
also Ausonius (Leipsic, 1886, pp. 52, 59), cited by Rhys, *The
Arthurian Legend*, p. 119, note 4.

[2] Brébeuf, *Relations des Jésuites*, 1636, pp. 100-102.

I

ruins " through that dolorous stroke." Pellam becomes
the maimed king, who can only be healed by the Holy
Grail.   Apparently Celtic myths of obscure antiquity
have been adapted in France, and interwoven with
fables about Joseph of Arimathea and Christian
mysteries.   It is not possible here to go into the com-
plicated learning of the subject.   In Malory, Balin, after
dealing the dolorous stroke, borrows a strange shield
from a knight, and, thus accoutred, meets his brother
Balan, who does not recognise him.   They fight, both
die and are buried in one tomb, and Galahad later
achieves the adventure of winning Balin's sword.   "Thus
endeth the tale of Balyn and of Balan, two brethren
born in Northumberland, good knights," says Malory,
simply, and unconscious of the strange mythological
medley under the coat armour of romance.

The materials, then, seemed confused and obdurate,
but Tennyson works them into the course of the fatal
love of Lancelot and Guinevere, and into the spiritual
texture of the Idylls.   Balin has been expelled from
Court for the wildness that gives him his name, *Balin
le Sauvage.*   He had buffeted a squire in hall.   He
and Balan await all challengers beside a well.   Arthur
encounters and dismounts them.   Balin devotes himself
to self-conquest.   Then comes tidings that Pellam, of
old leagued with Lot against Arthur, has taken to religion, collects relics, claims descent from Joseph of
Arimathea, and owns the sacred spear that pierced the
side of Christ.   But Garlon is with him, the knight

invisible, who appears to come from an Irish source, or at least has a parallel in Irish legend. This Garlon has an unknightly way of killing men by viewless blows from the rear. Balan goes to encounter Garlon. Balin remains, learning courtesy, modelling himself on Lancelot, and gaining leave to bear Guinevere's Crown Matrimonial for his cognisance,—which, of course, Balan does not know,—

" As golden earnest of a better life."

But Balin sees reason to think that Lancelot and Guinevere love even too well.

"Then chanced, one morning, that Sir Balin sat
Close-bower'd in that garden nigh the hall.
A walk of roses ran from door to door ;
A walk of lilies crost it to the bower :
And down that range of roses the great Queen
Came with slow steps, the morning on her face ;
And all in shadow from the counter door
Sir Lancelot as to meet her, then at once,
As if he saw not, glanced aside, and paced
The long white walk of lilies toward the bower.
Follow'd the Queen ; Sir Balin heard her 'Prince,
Art thou so little loyal to thy Queen,
As pass without good morrow to thy Queen?'
To whom Sir Lancelot with his eyes on earth,
'Fain would I still be loyal to the Queen.'
'Yea so,' she said, 'but so to pass me by—
So loyal scarce is loyal to thyself,
Whom all men rate the king of courtesy.
Let be : ye stand, fair lord, as in a dream.'

Then Lancelot with his hand among the flowers,
'Yea—for a dream. Last night methought I saw

That maiden Saint who stands with lily in hand
In yonder shrine. All round her prest the dark,
And all the light upon her silver face
Flow'd from the spiritual lily that she held.
Lo! these her emblems drew mine eyes—away:
For see, how perfect-pure! As light a flush
As hardly tints the blossom of the quince
Would mar their charm of stainless maidenhood.'

  'Sweeter to me,' she said, 'this garden rose
Deep-hued and many-folded! sweeter still
The wild-wood hyacinth and the bloom of May.
Prince, we have ridd'n before among the flowers
In those fair days—not all as cool as these,
Tho' season-earlier. Art thou sad? or sick?
Our noble King will send thee his own leech—
Sick? or for any matter anger'd at me?'

  Then Lancelot lifted his large eyes; they dwelt
Deep-tranced on hers, and could not fall: her hue
Changed at his gaze: so turning side by side
They past, and Balin started from his bower.

  'Queen? subject? but I see not what I see.
Damsel and lover? hear not what I hear.
My father hath begotten me in his wrath.
I suffer from the things before me, know,
Learn nothing; am not worthy to be knight;
A churl, a clown!' and in him gloom on gloom
Deepen'd: he sharply caught his lance and shield,
Nor stay'd to crave permission of the King,
But, mad for strange adventure, dash'd away."

Balin is "disillusioned," his faith in the Ideal is shaken
if not shattered. He rides at adventure. Arriving at
the half-ruined castle of Pellam, that dubious devotee,

he hears Garlon insult Guinevere, but restrains himself.
Next day, again insulted for bearing "the crown scandalous" on his shield, he strikes Garlon down, is pursued, seizes the sacred spear, and escapes. Vivien
meets him in the woods, drops scandal in his ears, and
so maddens him that he defaces his shield with the
crown of Guinevere. Her song, and her words,

> "This fire of Heaven,
> This old sun-worship, boy, will rise again,
> And beat the cross to earth, and break the King
> And all his Table,"

might be forced into an allegory of the revived pride of
life, at the Renaissance and after. The maddened yells
of Balin strike the ear of Balan, who thinks he has met
the foul knight Garlon, that

> "Tramples on the goodly shield to show
> His loathing of our Order and the Queen."

They fight, fatally wound, and finally recognise each
other : Balan trying to restore Balin's faith in Guinevere,
who is merely slandered by Garlon and Vivien. Balin
acknowledges that his wildness has been their common
bane, and they die, "either locked in either's arms."

There is nothing in Malory, nor in any other source,
so far as I am aware, which suggested to Tennyson the
clou of the situation—the use of Guinevere's crown as a
cognisance by Balin. This device enables the poet to
weave the rather confused and unintelligible adventures
of Balin and Balan into the scheme, and to make it a

stage in the progress of his fable. That Balin was reck-
less and wild Malory bears witness, but his endeavours to
conquer himself and reach the ideal set by Lancelot are
Tennyson's addition, with all the tragedy of Balin's dis-
enchantment and despair. The strange fantastic house
of Pellam, full of the most sacred things,

" In which he scarce could spy the Christ for Saints,"

yet sheltering the human fiend Garlon, is supplied by
Malory, whose predecessors probably blended more than
one myth of the old Cymry into the romance, washed
over with Christian colouring. As Malory tells this part
of the tale it is perhaps more strange and effective than
in the Idyll. The introduction of Vivien into this adventure is wholly due to Tennyson : her appearance here
leads up to her triumph in the poem which follows,
Merlin and Vivien.

The nature and origin of Merlin are something of a
mystery. Hints and rumours of Merlin, as of Arthur,
stream from hill and grave as far north as Tweedside.
If he was a historical person, myths of magic might
crystallise round him, as round Virgil in Italy. The
process would be the easier in a country where the
practices of Druidry still lingered, and revived after the
retreat of the Romans. The mediæval romancers invented a legend that Merlin was a virgin-born child of
Satan. In Tennyson he may be guessed to represent
the fabled esoteric lore of old religions, with their vague
pantheisms, and such magic as the *tapas* of Brahmanic

legends. He is wise with a riddling evasive wisdom : the builder of Camelot, the prophet, a shadow of Druidry clinging to the Christian king. His wisdom cannot avail him : if he beholds "his own mischance with a glassy countenance," he cannot avoid his shapen fate. He becomes assotted of Vivien, and goes open-eyed to his doom.

The enchantress, Vivien, is one of that dubious company of Ladies of the Lake, now friendly, now treacherous. Probably these ladies are the fairies of popular Celtic tradition, taken up into the more elaborate poetry of Cymric literature and mediæval romance. Mr Rhys traces Vivien, or Nimue, or Nyneue, back, through a series of palæographic changes and errors, to Rhiannon, wife of Pwyll, a kind of lady of the lake he thinks, but the identification is not very satisfactory. Vivien is certainly "one of the damsels of the lake" in Malory, and the damsels of the lake seem to be lake fairies, with all their beguilements and strange unstable loves. "And always Merlin lay about the lady to have her maidenhood, and she was ever passing weary of him, and fain would have been delivered of him, for she was afraid of him because he was a devil's son. . . . So by her subtle working she made Merlin to go under that stone to let her wit of the marvels there, but she wrought so there for him that he came never out for all the craft he could do. And so she departed and left Merlin." The sympathy of Malory is not with the enchanter. In the Idylls, as

finally published, Vivien is born on a battlefield of
death, with a nature perverted, and an instinctive hatred
of the good. Wherefore she leaves the Court of King
Mark to make mischief in Camelot. She is, in fact,
the ideal minx, a character not elsewhere treated by
Tennyson :—

> " She hated all the knights, and heard in thought
> Their lavish comment when her name was named.
> For once, when Arthur walking all alone,
> Vext at a rumour issued from herself
> Of some corruption crept among his knights,
> Had met her, Vivien, being greeted fair,
> Would fain have wrought upon his cloudy mood
> With reverent eyes mock-loyal, shaken voice,
> And flutter'd adoration, and at last
> With dark sweet hints of some who prized him more
> Than who should prize him most ; at which the King
> Had gazed upon her blankly and gone by :
> But one had watch'd, and had not held his peace :
> It made the laughter of an afternoon
> That Vivien should attempt the blameless King.
> And after that, she set herself to gain
> Him, the most famous man of all those times,
> Merlin, who knew the range of all their arts,
> Had built the King his havens, ships, and halls,
> Was also Bard, and knew the starry heavens ;
> The people call'd him Wizard ; whom at first
> She play'd about with slight and sprightly talk,
> And vivid smiles, and faintly-venom'd points
> Of slander, glancing here and grazing there ;
> And yielding to his kindlier moods, the Seer
> Would watch her at her petulance, and play,
> Ev'n when they seem'd unloveable, and laugh
> As those that watch a kitten ; thus he grew
> Tolerant of what he half disdain'd, and she,

Perceiving that she was but half disdain'd,
Began to break her sports with graver fits,
Turn red or pale, would often when they met
Sigh fully, or all-silent gaze upon him.
With such a fixt devotion, that the old man,
Tho' doubtful, felt the flattery, and at times
Would flatter his own wish in age for love,
And half believe her true : for thus at times
He waver'd ; but that other clung to him,
Fixt in her will, and so the seasons went."

Vivien is modern enough—if any type of character is modern : at all events there is no such Blanche Amory of a girl in the old legends and romances. In these Merlin fatigues the lady by his love ; she learns his arts, and gets rid of him as she can. His forebodings in the Idyll contain a magnificent image :—

"There lay she all her length and kiss'd his feet,
As if in deepest reverence and in love.
A twist of gold was round her hair ; a robe
Of samite without price, that more exprest
Than hid her, clung about her lissome limbs,
In colour like the satin-shining palm
On sallows in the windy gleams of March :
And while she kiss'd them, crying, ' Trample me,
Dear feet, that I have follow'd thro' the world,
And I will pay you worship ; tread me down
And I will kiss you for it' ; he was mute :
So dark a forethought roll'd about his brain,
As on a dull day in an Ocean cave
The blind wave feeling round his long sea-hall
In silence."

We think of the blinded Cyclops groping round his cave, like "the blind wave feeling round his long sea-hall."

The richness, the many shining contrasts and immortal lines in *Vivien*, seem almost too noble for a
subject not ..asily redeemed, and the picture of the
ideal Court lying in full corruption.   Next to *Elaine*,
Jowett wrote that he " admired *Vivien* the most (the
naughty one), which seems to me a work of wonderful power and skill.   It is most elegant and fanci-
ful.   I am not surprised at your Delilah beguiling the
wise man ; she is quite equal to it."   The dramatic
versatility of Tennyson's genius, his power of creating
the most various characters, is nowhere better displayed
than in the contrast between the *Vivien* and the *Elaine*.
Vivien is a type, her adventure is of a nature, which he
has not elsewhere handled.   Thackeray, who admired
the Idylls so enthusiastically, might have recognised in
Vivien a character not unlike some of his own, as dark
as Becky Sharp, more terrible in her selfishness than
that Beatrix Esmond who is still a paragon, and, in her
creator's despite, a queen of hearts.   In Elaine, on the
other hand, Tennyson has drawn a girl so innocently
passionate, and told a tale of love that never found his
earthly close, so delicately beautiful, that we may perhaps
place this Idyll the highest of his poems on love, and
reckon it the gem of the Idylls, the central diamond in
the diamond crown.   Reading *Elaine* once more, after
an interval of years, one is captivated by its grace, its
pathos, its nobility.   The poet had touched on some
unidentified form of the story, long before, in *The Lady
of Shalott*.   That poem had the mystery of romance,

but, in human interest, could not compete with *Elaine*, if indeed any poem of Tennyson's can be ranked with this matchless Idyll.

The mere invention, and, as we may say, *charpentage*, are of the first order. The materials in Malory, though beautiful, are simple, and left a field for the poet's invention.[1]

Arthur, with the Scots and Northern knights, means to encounter all comers at a Whitsuntide tourney. Guinevere is ill, and cannot go to the jousts, while Lancelot makes excuse that he is not healed of a wound. "Wherefore the King was heavy and passing wroth, and so he departed towards Winchester." The Queen then blamed Lancelot : people will say they deceive Arthur. "Madame," said Sir Lancelot, " I allow your wit ; it is of late come that ye were wise." In the Idyll Guinevere speaks as if their early loves had been as conspicuous as, according to George Buchanan, were those of Queen Mary and Bothwell. Lancelot will go to the tourney, and, despite Guinevere's warning, will take part against Arthur and his own fierce Northern kinsmen. He rides to Astolat—"that is, Gylford"—where Arthur sees him. He borrows the blank shield of " Sir Torre," and the company of his brother Sir Lavaine. Elaine "cast such a love unto Sir Lancelot that she would never withdraw her love, wherefore she died." At her prayer, and for better disguise (as he had never worn a lady's favour), Lancelot carried her scarlet pearl-em-

[1] Malory, xviii. 8 *et seq.*

broidered sleeve in his helmet, and left his shield in
Elaine's keeping.   The tourney passes as in the poem,
Gawain recognising Lancelot, but puzzled by the favour
he wears.   The wounded Lancelot "thought to do what
he might while he might endure."   When he is offered
the prize he is so sore hurt that he "takes no force of
no honour."   He rides into a wood, where Lavaine
draws forth the spear.   Lavaine brings Lancelot to
the hermit, once a knight.   "I have seen the day,"
says the hermit, "I would have loved him the worse,
because he was against my lord, King Arthur, for
some time.   I was one of the fellowship of the
Round Table, but I thank God now I am otherwise disposed."   Gawain, seeking the wounded knight,
comes to Astolat, where Elaine declares "he is the
man in the world that I first loved, and truly he is
the last that ever I shall love."   Gawain, on seeing the
shield, tells Elaine that the wounded knight is Lancelot,
and she goes to seek him and Lavaine.   Gawain does
not pay court to Elaine, nor does Arthur rebuke him, as
in the poem.   When Guinevere heard that Lancelot bore
another lady's favour, "she was nigh out of her mind
for wrath," and expressed her anger to Sir Bors, for
Gawain had spoken of the maid of Astolat.   Bors tells
this to Lancelot, who is tended by Elaine.   " 'But I
well see,' said Sir Bors, 'by her diligence about you that
she loveth you entirely.'   'That me repenteth,' said Sir
Lancelot.   Said Sir Bors, 'Sir, she is not the first that
hath lost her pain upon you, and that is the more pity.' "

When Lancelot recovers, and returns to Astolat, she declares her love with the frankness of ladies in mediæval romance. " Have mercy upon me and suffer me not to die for thy love." Lancelot replies with the courtesy and the offers of service which became him. "Of all this," said the maiden, " I will none ; for but if ye will wed me, or be my paramour at the least, wit you well, Sir Lancelot, my good days are done."

This was a difficult pass for the poet, living in other days of other manners. His art appears in the turn which he gives to Elaine's declaration :—

> " But when Sir Lancelot's deadly hurt was whole,
> To Astolat returning rode the three.
> There morn by morn, arraying her sweet self
> In that wherein she deem'd she look'd her best,
> She came before Sir Lancelot, for she thought
> ' If I be loved, these are my festal robes,
> If not, the victim's flowers before he fall.'
> And Lancelot ever prest upon the maid
> That she should ask some goodly gift of him
> For her own self or hers ; ' and do not shun
> To speak the wish most near to your true heart ;
> Such service have ye done me, that I make
> My will of yours, and Prince and Lord am I
> In mine own land, and what I will I can.'
> Then like a ghost she lifted up her face,
> But like a ghost without the power to speak.
> And Lancelot saw that she withheld her wish,
> And bode among them yet a little space
> Till he should learn it ; and one morn it chanced
> He found her in among the garden yews,
> And said, ' Delay no longer, speak your wish,
> Seeing I go to-day ' : then out she brake :

'Going? and we shall never see you more.
And I must die for want of one bold word.'
'Speak : that I live to hear,' he said, 'is yours.'
Then suddenly and passionately she spoke :
'I have gone mad.   I love you : let me die.'
'Ah, sister,' answer'd Lancelot, 'what is this?'
And innocently extending her white arms,
'Your love,' she said, 'your love—to be your wife.'
And Lancelot answer'd, 'Had I chosen to wed,
I had been wedded earlier, sweet Elaine :
But now there never will be wife of mine.'
'No, no,' she cried, 'I care not to be wife,
But to be with you still, to see your face,
To serve you, and to follow you thro' the world.'
And Lancelot answer'd, 'Nay, the world, the world,
All ear and eye, with such a stupid heart
To interpret ear and eye, and such a tongue
To blare its own interpretation—nay,
Full ill then should I quit your brother's love,
And your good father's kindness.'   And she said,
'Not to be with you, not to see your face—
Alas for me then, my good days are done.'"

So she dies, and is borne down Thames to London, the fairest corpse, "and she lay as though she had smiled." Her letter is read. "Ye might have showed her," said the Queen, "some courtesy and gentleness that might have preserved her life ;" and so the two are reconciled.

Such, in brief, is the tender old tale of true love, with the shining courtesy of Lavaine and the father of the maid, who speak no word of anger against Lancelot. "For since first I saw my lord, Sir Lancelot," says Lavaine, "I could never depart from him, nor nought I

will, if I may follow him : she doth as I do." To the
simple and moving story Tennyson adds, by way of
ornament, the diamonds, the prize of the tourney, and
the manner of their finding :—

"For Arthur, long before they crown'd him King,
Roving the trackless realms of Lyonnesse,
Had found a glen, gray boulder and black tarn.
A horror lived about the tarn, and clave
Like its own mists to all the mountain side :
For here two brothers, one a king, had met
And fought together ; but their names were lost ;
And each had slain his brother at a blow ;
And down they fell and made the glen abhorr'd :
And there they lay till all their bones were bleach'd,
And lichen'd into colour with the crags :
And he, that once was king, had on a crown
Of diamonds, one in front, and four aside.
And Arthur came, and labouring up the pass,
All in a misty moonshine, unawares
Had trodden that crown'd skeleton, and the skull
Brake from the nape, and from the skull the crown
Roll'd into light, and turning on its rims
Fled like a glittering rivulet to the tarn :
And down the shingly scaur he plunged, and caught,
And set it on his head, and in his heart
Heard murmurs, ' Lo, thou likewise shalt be King.'"

The diamonds reappear in the scene of Guinevere's
jealousy :—

"All in an oriel on the summer side,
Vine-clad, of Arthur's palace toward the stream,
They met, and Lancelot kneeling utter'd, 'Queen,
Lady, my liege, in whom I have my joy,
Take, what I had not won except for you,
These jewels, and make me happy, making them

An armlet for the roundest arm on earth,
Or necklace for a neck to which the swan's
Is tawnier than her cygnet's : these are words :
Your beauty is your beauty, and I sin
In speaking, yet O grant my worship of it
Words, as we grant grief tears.   Such sin in words,
Perchance, we both can pardon : but, my Queen,
I hear of rumours flying thro' your court.
Our bond, as not the bond of man and wife,
Should have in it an absoluter trust
To make up that defect : let rumours be :
When did not rumours fly ? these, as I trust
That you trust me in your own nobleness,
I may not well believe that you believe.'

   While thus he spoke, half turn'd away, the Queen
Brake from the vast oriel-embowering vine
Leaf after leaf, and tore, and cast them off,
Till all the place whereon she stood was green ;
Then, when he ceased, in one cold passive hand
Received at once and laid aside the gems
There on a table near her, and replied :

   'It may be, I am quicker of belief
Than you believe me, Lancelot of the Lake.
Our bond is not the bond of man and wife.
This good is in it, whatsoe'er of ill,
It can be broken easier.   I for you
This many a year have done despite and wrong
To one whom ever in my heart of hearts
I did acknowledge nobler.   What are these ?
Diamonds for me ! they had been thrice their worth
Being your gift, had you not lost your own.
To loyal hearts the value of all gifts
Must vary as the giver's.   Not for me !
For her ! for your new fancy.   Only this
Grant me, I pray you : have your joys apart.

I doubt not that however changed, you keep
So much of what is graceful : and myself
Would shun to break those bounds of courtesy
In which as Arthur's Queen I move and rule :
So cannot speak my mind.   An end to this !
A strange one ! yet I take it with Amen.
So pray you, add my diamonds to her pearls ;
Deck her with these ; tell her, she shines me down :
An armlet for an arm to which the Queen's
Is haggard, or a necklace for a neck
O as much fairer—as a faith once fair
Was richer than these diamonds—hers not mine—
Nay, by the mother of our Lord himself,
Or hers or mine, mine now to work my will—
She shall not have them.'

                     Saying which she seized,
And, thro' the casement standing wide for heat,
Flung them, and down they flash'd, and smote the stream.
Then from the smitten surface flash'd, as it were,
Diamonds to meet them, and they past away.
Then while Sir Lancelot leant, in half disdain
At love, life, all things, on the window ledge,
Close underneath his eyes, and right across
Where these had fallen, slowly past the barge
Whereon the lily maid of Astolat
Lay smiling, like a star in blackest night."

This affair of the diamonds is the chief addition to the old tale, in which we already see the curse of lawless love, fallen upon the jealous Queen and the long-enduring Lancelot. "This is not the first time," said Sir Lancelot, "that ye have been displeased with me causeless, but, madame, ever I must suffer you, but what sorrow I endure I take no force" (that is, " I disregard ").

The romance, and the poet, in his own despite, cannot but make Lancelot the man we love, not Arthur or another. Human nature perversely sides with Guinevere against the Blameless King :—

> " She broke into a little scornful laugh :
> 'Arthur, my lord, Arthur, the faultless King,
> That passionate perfection, my good lord—
> But who can gaze upon the Sun in heaven?
> He never spake word of reproach to me,
> He never had a glimpse of mine untruth,
> He cares not for me : only here to-day
> There gleam'd a vague suspicion in his eyes :
> Some meddling rogue has tamper'd with him—else
> Rapt in this fancy of his Table Round,
> And swearing men to vows impossible,
> To make them like himself : but, friend, to me
> He is all fault who hath no fault at all :
> For who loves me must have a touch of earth ;
> The low sun makes the colour : I am yours,
> Not Arthur's, as ye know, save by the bond."

It is not the beautiful Queen who wins us, our hearts are with " the innocence of love " in Elaine. But Lancelot has the charm that captivated Lavaine ; and Tennyson's Arthur remains

> " The moral child without the craft to rule,
> Else had he not lost me."

Indeed the romance of Malory makes Arthur deserve " the pretty popular name such manhood earns " by his conduct as regards Guinevere when she is accused by her enemies in the later chapters. Yet Malory does not finally condone the sin which baffles Lancelot's quest of the Holy Grail.

Tennyson at first was in doubt as to writing on the Grail, for certain respects of reverence. When he did approach the theme it was in a method of extreme condensation. The romances on the Grail outrun the length even of mediæval poetry and prose. They are exceedingly confused, as was natural, if that hypothesis which regards the story as a Christianised form of obscure Celtic myth be correct. Sir Percivale's sister, in the Idyll, has the first vision of the Grail :—

> "Sweet brother, I have seen the Holy Grail :
> For, waked at dead of night, I heard a sound
> As of a silver horn from o'er the hills
> Blown, and I thought, 'It is not Arthur's use
> To hunt by moonlight'; and the slender sound
> As from a distance beyond distance grew
> Coming upon me—O never harp nor horn,
> Nor aught we blow with breath, or touch with hand,
> Was like that music as it came ; and then
> Stream'd thro' my cell a cold and silver beam,
> And down the long beam stole the Holy Grail,
> Rose-red with beatings in it, as if alive,
> Till all the white walls of my cell were dyed
> With rosy colours leaping on the wall ;
> And then the music faded, and the Grail
> Past, and the beam decay'd, and from the walls
> The rosy quiverings died into the night.
> So now the Holy Thing is here again
> Among us, brother, fast thou too and pray,
> And tell thy brother knights to fast and pray,
> That so perchance the vision may be seen
> By thee and those, and all the world be heal'd."

Galahad, son of Lancelot and the first Elaine (who became Lancelot's mistress by art magic), then vows

himself to the Quest, and, after the vision in hall at
Camelot, the knights, except Arthur, follow his example,
to Arthur's grief.   "Ye follow wandering fires!"   Probably, or perhaps, the poet indicates dislike of hasty
spiritual enthusiasms, of "seeking for a sign," and of the
mysticism which betokens want of faith.   The Middle
Ages, more than many readers know, were ages of doubt.
Men desired the witness of the senses to the truth of
what the Church taught, they wished to see that naked
child of the romance "smite himself into" the wafer
of the Sacrament.   The author of the *Imitatio Christi*
discourages such vain and too curious inquiries as helped
to rend the Church, and divided Christendom into hostile
camps.   The Quest of the actual Grail was a knightly
form of theological research into the unsearchable;
undertaken, often in a secular spirit of adventure, by
sinful men.   The poet's heart is rather with human
things :—

> "'O brother,' ask'd Ambrosius,—'for in sooth
> These ancient books—and they would win thee—teem,
> Only I find not there this Holy Grail,
> With miracles and marvels like to these,
> Not all unlike ; which oftentime I read,
> Who read but on my breviary with ease,
> Till my head swims ; and then go forth and pass
> Down to the little thorpe that lies so close,
> And almost plaster'd like a martin's nest
> To these old walls—and mingle with our folk ;
> And knowing every honest face of theirs
> As well as ever shepherd knew his sheep,
> And every homely secret in their hearts,

Delight myself with gossip and old wives,
And ills and aches, and teethings, lyings-in,
And mirthful sayings, children of the place,
That have no meaning half a league away :
Or lulling random squabbles when they rise,
Chafferings and chatterings at the market-cross,
Rejoice, small man, in this small world of mine,
Yea, even in their hens and in their eggs.'"

This appears to be Tennyson's original reading of the
Quest of the Grail. His own mysticism, which did not
strive, or cry, or seek after marvels, though marvels
might come unsought, is expressed in Arthur's words :—

"'"And spake I not too truly, O my knights?
Was I too dark a prophet when I said
To those who went upon the Holy Quest,
That most of them would follow wandering fires,
Lost in the quagmire?—lost to me and gone,
And left me gazing at a barren board,
And a lean Order—scarce return'd a tithe—
And out of those to whom the vision came
My greatest hardly will believe he saw ;
Another hath beheld it afar off,
And leaving human wrongs to right themselves,
Cares but to pass into the silent life.
And one hath had the vision face to face,
And now his chair desires him here in vain,
However they may crown him otherwhere.

'"And some among you held, that if the King
Had seen the sight he would have sworn the vow :
Not easily, seeing that the King must guard
That which he rules, and is but as the hind
To whom a space of land is given to plow
Who may not wander from the allotted field
Before his work be done ; but, being done,

Let visions of the night or of the day
Come, as they will; and many a time they come,
Until this earth he walks on seems not earth,
This light that strikes his eyeball is not light,
This air that smites his forehead is not air
But vision—yea, his very hand and foot—
In moments when he feels he cannot die,
And knows himself no vision to himself,
Nor the high God a vision, nor that One
Who rose again : ye have seen what ye have seen."

'So spake the King : I knew not all he meant.'"

The closing lines declare, as far as the poet could
declare them, these subjective experiences of his which,
in a manner rarely parallelled, coloured and formed his
thought on the highest things. He introduces them
even into this poem on a topic which, because of its
sacred associations, he for long did not venture to touch.

In *Pelleas and Ettarre*—which deals with the sorrows
of one of the young knights who fill up the gaps left at
the Round Table by the mischances of the Quest—it
would be difficult to trace a Celtic original. For
Malory, not Celtic legend, supplied Tennyson with
the germinal idea of a poem which, in the romance,
has no bearing on the final catastrophe. Pelleas, a
King of the Isles, loves the beautiful Ettarre, "a
great lady," and for her wins at a tourney the prize of
the golden circlet. But she hates and despises him,
and Sir Gawain is a spectator when, as in the poem,
the felon knights of Ettarre bind and insult their
conqueror, Pelleas. Gawain promises to win the love

of Ettarre for Pelleas, and, as in the poem, borrows his arms and horse, and pretends to have slain him. But in place of turning Ettarre's heart towards Pelleas, Gawain becomes her lover, and Pelleas, detecting them asleep, lays his naked sword on their necks. He then rides home to die ; but Nimue (Vivien), the Lady of the Lake, restores him to health and sanity.   His fever gone, he scorns Ettarre, who, by Nimue's enchantment, now loves him as much as she had hated him.   Pelleas weds Nimue, and Ettarre dies of a broken heart.   Tennyson, of course, could not make Nimue (his Vivien) do anything benevolent.   He therefore closes his poem by a repetition of the effect in the case of Balin.   Pelleas is driven desperate by the treachery of Gawain, the reported infidelity of Guinevere, and the general corruption of the ideal.   A shadow falls on Lancelot and Guinevere, and Modred sees that his hour is drawing nigh.   In spite of beautiful passages this is not one of the finest of the Idylls, save for the study of the fierce, hateful, and beautiful *grande dame*, Ettarre.   The narrative does little to advance the general plot.   In the original of Malory it has no connection with the Lancelot cycle, except as far as it reveals the treachery of Gawain, the gay and fair-spoken "light of love," brother of the traitor Modred.   A simpler treatment of the theme may be read in Mr Swinburne's beautiful poem, *The Tale of Balen.*

It is in *The Last Tournament* that Modred finds the beginning of his opportunity.   The brief life of the

Ideal has burned itself out, as the year, in its vernal
beauty when Arthur came, is burning out in autumn.
The poem is purposely autumnal, with the autumn, not
of mellow fruitfulness, but of the "flying gold of the
ruined woodlands" and the dank odours of decay. In
that miserable season is held the Tourney of the Dead
Innocence, with the blood-red prize of rubies. With
a wise touch Tennyson has represented the Court as
fallen not into vice only and crime, but into positive
vulgarity and bad taste. The Tournament is a carnival
of the "smart" and the third-rate. Courtesy is dead,
even Tristram is brutal, and in Iseult hatred of her
husband is as powerful as love of her lover. The
satire strikes at England, where the world has never
been corrupt with a good grace. It is a passage of
arms neither gentle nor joyous that Lancelot presides
over :—

> "The sudden trumpet sounded as in a dream
> To ears but half-awaked, then one low roll
> Of Autumn thunder, and the jousts began :
> And ever the wind blew, and yellowing leaf
> And gloom and gleam, and shower and shorn plume
> Went down it. Sighing weariedly, as one
> Who sits and gazes on a faded fire,
> When all the goodlier guests are past away,
> Sat their great umpire, looking o'er the lists.
> He saw the laws that ruled the tournament
> Broken, but spake not ; once, a knight cast down
> Before his throne of arbitration cursed
> The dead babe and the follies of the King ;
> And once the laces of a helmet crack'd,

And show'd him, like a vermin in its hole,
Modred, a narrow face : anon he heard
The voice that billow'd round the barriers roar
An ocean-sounding welcome to one knight,
But newly-enter'd, taller than the rest,
And armour'd all in forest green, whereon
There tript a hundred tiny silver deer,
And wearing but a holly-spray for crest,
With ever-scattering berries, and on shield
A spear, a harp, a bugle—Tristram—late
From overseas in Brittany return'd,
And marriage with a princess of that realm,
Isolt the White—Sir Tristram of the Woods—
Whom Lancelot knew, had held sometime with pain
His own against him, and now yearn'd to shake
The burthen off his heart in one full shock
With Tristram ev'n to death : his strong hands gript
And dinted the gilt dragons right and left,
Until he groan'd for wrath—so many of those,
That ware their ladies' colours on the casque,
Drew from before Sir Tristram to the bounds,
And there with gibes and flickering mockeries
Stood, while he mutter'd, 'Craven crests ! O shame !
What faith have these in whom they sware to love ?
The glory of our Round Table is no more.'

So Tristram won, and Lancelot gave, the gems,
Not speaking other word than ' Hast thou won ?
Art thou the purest, brother ?   See, the hand
Wherewith thou takest this, is red !' to whom
Tristram, half plagued by Lancelot's languorous mood,
Made answer, 'Ay, but wherefore toss me this
Like a dry bone cast to some hungry hound ?
Let be thy fair Queen's fantasy.   Strength of heart
And might of limb, but mainly use and skill,
Are winners in this pastime of our King.
My hand—belike the lance hath dript upon it—

No blood of mine, I trow ; but O chief knight,
Right arm of Arthur in the battlefield,
Great brother, thou nor I have made the world ;
Be happy in thy fair Queen as I in mine.'

 And Tristram round the gallery made his horse
Caracole ; then bow'd his homage, bluntly saying,
' Fair damsels, each to him who worships each
Sole Queen of Beauty and of love, behold
This day my Queen of Beauty is not here.'
And most of these were mute, some anger'd, one
Murmuring, ' All courtesy is dead,' and one,
' The glory of our Round Table is no more.'

 Then fell thick rain, plume droopt and mantle clung,
And pettish cries awoke, and the wan day
Went glooming down in wet and weariness :
But under her black brows a swarthy one
Laugh'd shrilly, crying, ' Praise the patient saints,
Our one white day of Innocence hath past,
Tho' somewhat draggled at the skirt. So be it.
The snowdrop only, flowering thro' the year,
Would make the world as blank as Winter-tide.
Come—let us gladden their sad eyes, our Queen's
And Lancelot's, at this night's solemnity
With all the kindlier colours of the field.' "

Arthur's last victory over a robber knight is ingloriously
squalid :—

 " He ended : Arthur knew the voice ; the face
Wellnigh was helmet-hidden, and the name
Went wandering somewhere darkling in his mind.
And Arthur deign'd not use of word or sword,
But let the drunkard, as he stretch'd from horse
To strike him, overbalancing his bulk,
Down from the causeway heavily to the swamp

Fall, as the crest of some slow-arching wave,
Heard in dead night along that table-shore,
Drops flat, and after the great waters break
Whitening for half a league, and thin themselves,
Far over sands marbled with moon and cloud,
From less and less to nothing ; thus he fell
Head-heavy ; then the knights, who watch'd him, roar'd
And shouted and leapt down upon the fall'n ;
There trampled out his face from being known,
And sank his head in mire, and slimed themselves :
Nor heard the King for their own cries, but sprang
Thro' open doors, and swording right and left
Men, women, on their sodden faces, hurl'd
The tables over and the wines, and slew
Till all the rafters rang with woman-yells,
And all the pavement stream'd with massacre :
Then, echoing yell with yell, they fired the tower,
Which half that autumn night, like the live North,
Red-pulsing up thro' Alioth and Alcor,
Made all above it, and a hundred meres
About it, as the water Moab saw
Come round by the East, and out beyond them flush'd
The long low dune, and lazy-plunging sea."

Guinevere is one of the greatest of the Idylls.
Malory makes Lancelot more sympathetic ; his fight,
unarmed, in Guinevere's chamber, against the felon
knights, is one of his most spirited scenes. Tennyson
omits this, and omits all the unpardonable behaviour of
Arthur as narrated in Malory. Critics have usually
condemned the last parting of Guinevere and Arthur,
because the King doth preach too much to an unhappy
woman who has no reply. The position of Arthur is
not easily redeemable : it is difficult to conceive that

a noble nature could be, or should be, blind so long.
He does rehabilitate his Queen in her own self-respect,
perhaps, by assuring her that he loves her still :—

"Let no man dream but that I love thee still."

Had he said that one line and no more, we might have
loved him better.　In the Idylls we have not Malory's
last meeting of Lancelot and Guinevere, one of the
scenes in which the wandering composite romance
ends as nobly as the *Iliad*.

The Passing of Arthur, except for a new introductory
passage of great beauty and appropriateness, is the
Morte d'Arthur, first published in 1842 :—

"So all day long the noise of battle roll'd
　Among the mountains by the winter sea."

The year has run its course, spring, summer, gloomy
autumn, and dies in the mist of Arthur's last wintry
battle in the west—

"And the new sun rose, bringing the new year."

The splendid and sombre procession has passed, leaving
us to muse as to how far the poet has fulfilled his own
ideal.　There could be no new epic : he gave a chain of
heroic Idylls.　An epic there could not be, for the *Iliad*
and *Odyssey* have each a unity of theme, a narrative
compressed into a few days in the former, in the latter
into forty days of time.　The tragedy of Arthur's reign
could not so be condensed ; and Tennyson chose the

only feasible plan. He has left a work, not absolutely perfect, indeed, but such as he conceived, after many tentative essays, and such as he desired to achieve. His fame may not rest chiefly on the Idylls, but they form one of the fairest jewels in the crown that shines with unnumbered gems, each with its own glory.

VIII.

ENOCH ARDEN. THE DRAMAS.

THE success of the first volume of the Idylls recom-
pensed the poet for the slings and arrows that gave
Maud a hostile welcome.   His next publication was the
beautiful *Tithonus*, a fit pendant to the *Ulysses*, and composed about the same date (1833-35).   "A quarter of a
century ago," Tennyson dates it, writing in 1860 to the
Duke of Argyll.   He had found it when "ferreting
among my old books," he said, in search of something
for Thackeray, who was establishing the *Cornhill
Magazine*.   What must the wealth of the poet have
been, who, possessing *Tithonus* in his portfolio, did not
take the trouble to insert it in the volumes of 1842 !
Nobody knows how many poems of Tennyson's never
even saw pen and ink, being composed unwritten, and
forgotten.   At this time we find him recommending Mr
Browning's *Men and Women* to the Duke, who, like
many Tennysonians, does not seem to have been a ready
convert to his great contemporary.   The Duke and
Duchess urged the Laureate to attempt the topic of the

Holy Grail, but he was not in the mood. Indeed the vision of the Grail in the early *Sir Galahad* is doubtless happier than the allegorical handling of a theme so obscure, remote, and difficult, in the Idylls. He wrote his *Boadicea*, a piece magnificent in itself, but of difficult popular access, owing to the metrical experiment.

In the autumn of 1860 he revisited Cornwall with F. T. Palgrave, Mr Val Prinsep, and Mr Holman Hunt. They walked in the rain, saw Tintagel and the Scilly Isles, and were fêted by an enthusiastic captain of a little river steamer, who was more interested in " Mr Tinman and Mr Pancake " than the Celtic boatman of Ardtornish. The winter was passed at Farringford, and the *Northern Farmer* was written there, a Lincolnshire reminiscence, in the February of 1861. In autumn the Pyrenees were visited by Tennyson in company with Arthur Clough and Mr Dakyns of Clifton College. At Cauteretz in August, and among memories of the old tour with Arthur Hallam, was written *All along the Valley*. The ways, however, in Auvergne were " foul," and the diet " unhappy." The dedication of the Idylls was written on the death of the Prince Consort in December, and in January 1862 the Ode for the opening of an exhibition. The poet was busy with his "Fisherman," *Enoch Arden*. The volume was published in 1864, and Lord Tennyson says it has been, next to *In Memoriam*, the most popular of his father's works. One would have expected the one volume containing the poems up to 1842 to hold that place.

The new book, however, mainly dealt with English, contemporary, and domestic themes—"the poetry of the
affections." An old woman, a district visitor reported,
regarded *Enoch Arden* as "more beautiful" than the
other tracts which were read to her. It is indeed a
tender and touching tale, based on a folk-story which
Tennyson found current in Brittany as well as in England. Nor is the unseen and unknown landscape of the
tropic isle less happily created by the poet's imagination
than the familiar English cliffs and hazel copses :—

> "The mountain wooded to the peak, the lawns
> And winding glades high up like ways to Heaven,
> The slender coco's drooping crown of plumes,
> The lightning flash of insect and of bird,
> The lustre of the long convolvuluses
> That coil'd around the stately stems, and ran
> Ev'n to the limit of the land, the glows
> And glories of the broad belt of the world,
> All these he saw ; but what he fain had seen
> He could not see, the kindly human face,
> Nor ever hear a kindly voice, but heard
> The myriad shriek of wheeling ocean-fowl,
> The league-long roller thundering on the reef,
> The moving whisper of huge trees that branch'd
> And blossom'd in the zenith, or the sweep
> Of some precipitous rivulet to the wave,
> As down the shore he ranged, or all day long
> Sat often in the seaward-gazing gorge,
> A shipwreck'd sailor, waiting for a sail :
> No sail from day to day, but every day
> The sunrise broken into scarlet shafts
> Among the palms and ferns and precipices ;
> The blaze upon the waters to the east ;

The blaze upon his island overhead ;
The blaze upon the waters to the west ;
Then the great stars that globed themselves in Heaven,
The hollower-bellowing ocean, and again
The scarlet shafts of sunrise—but no sail."

Aylmer's Field somewhat recalls the burden of *Maud*,
the curse of purse-proud wealth, but is too gloomy to be
a fair specimen of Tennyson's art.   In *Sea Dreams* (first
published in 1860) the awful vision of crumbling faiths
is somewhat out of harmony with its environment :—

"But round the North, a light,
A belt, it seem'd, of luminous vapour, lay,
And ever in it a low musical note
Swell'd up and died ; and, as it swell'd, a ridge
Of breaker issued from the belt, and still
Grew with the growing note, and when the note
Had reach'd a thunderous fulness, on those cliffs
Broke, mixt with awful light (the same as that
Living within the belt) whereby she saw
That all those lines of cliffs were cliffs no more,
But huge cathedral fronts of every age,
Grave, florid, stern, as far as eye could see,
One after one : and then the great ridge drew,
Lessening to the lessening music, back,
And past into the belt and swell'd again
Slowly to music : ever when it broke
The statues, king or saint or founder fell ;
Then from the gaps and chasms of ruin left
Came men and women in dark clusters round,
Some crying, ' Set them up ! they shall not fall ! '
And others, ' Let them lie, for they have fall'n.'
And still they strove and wrangled : and she grieved
In her strange dream, she knew not why, to find
Their wildest wailings never out of tune

L

With that sweet note ; and ever as their shrieks
Ran highest up the gamut, that great wave
Returning, while none mark'd it, on the crowd
Broke, mixt with awful light, and show'd their eyes
Glaring, and passionate looks, and swept away
The men of flesh and blood, and men of stone,
To the waste deeps together.

                              'Then I fixt
My wistful eyes on two fair images,
Both crown'd with stars and high among the stars,—
The Virgin Mother standing with her child
High up on one of those dark minster-fronts—
Till she began to totter, and the child
Clung to the mother, and sent out a cry
Which mixt with little Margaret's, and I woke,
And my dream awed me :—well—but what are dreams?'"

The passage is rather fitted for a despairing mood of
Arthur, in the Idylls, than for the wife of the city clerk
ruined by a pious rogue.

The *Lucretius*, later published, is beyond praise as a
masterly study of the great Roman sceptic, whose heart
is at eternal odds with his Epicurean creed. Nascent
madness, or fever of the brain drugged by the blunder-
ing love philtre, is not more cunningly treated in the mad
scenes of *Maud*. No prose commentary on the *De
Rerum Natura*, however long and learned, conveys so
clearly as this concise study in verse the sense of mag
nificent mingled ruin in the mind and poem of the
Roman.

The " Experiments in Quantity " were, perhaps, suggested by Mr Matthew Arnold's Lectures on the Trans-

lating of Homer. Mr Arnold believed in a translation into English hexameters. His negative criticism of other translators and translations was amusing and instructive : he had an easy game to play with the Yankee-doodle metre of F. W. Newman, the ponderous blank verse of Cowper, the tripping and clipping couplets of Pope, the Elizabethan fantasies of Chapman. But **Mr** Arnold's hexameters were neither musical nor rapid : they only exhibited a new form of failure. As the Prince of Abyssinia said to his tutor, " Enough ; you have convinced me that no man can be a poet," so Mr Arnold went some way to prove that no man can **trans-**late Homer.

Tennyson had the lowest opinion of hexameters as an English metre for serious purposes.

> " These lame hexameters the strong - wing'd **music of** Homer ! "

Lord Tennyson says, " German hexameters he disliked even more than English." Indeed there is not much room for preference. Tennyson's Alcaics (*Milton*) were intended to follow the Greek rather than the Horatian model, and resulted, at all events, in a poem worthy of the " mighty - mouth'd inventor of harmonies." The specimen of the *Iliad* in blank verse, beautiful as it is, does not, somehow, reproduce the music of Homer. **It** is entirely Tennysonian, as in

> " Roll'd the rich vapour far into the heaven."

The reader, in that one line, recognises the voice **and**

trick of the English poet, and is far away from the
Chian :—

> "As when in heaven the stars about the moon
>   Look beautiful, when all the winds are laid,
>   And every height comes out, and jutting peak
>   And valley, and the immeasurable heavens
>   Break open to their highest, and all the stars
>   Shine, and the Shepherd gladdens in his heart :
>   So many a fire between the ships and stream
>   Of Xanthus blazed before the towers of Troy,
>   A thousand on the plain ; and close by each
>   Sat fifty in the blaze of burning fire ;
>   And eating hoary grain and pulse the steeds,
>   Fixt by their cars, waited the golden dawn."

This is excellent, is poetry, escapes the conceits of Pope
(who never "wrote with his eye on the object"), but is
pure Tennyson. We have not yet, probably we never
shall have, an adequate rendering of the *Iliad* into verse,
and prose translations do not pretend to be adequate.
When parents and dominies have abolished the study of
Greek, something, it seems, will have been lost to the
world, — something which even Tennyson could not
restore in English. He thought blank verse the proper
equivalent ; but it is no equivalent. One even prefers
his own prose :—

Nor did Paris linger in his lofty halls, but when he had
girt on his gorgeous armour, all of varied bronze, then he
rushed thro' the city, glorying in his airy feet. And as
when a stall-kept horse, that is barley-fed at the manger,
breaketh his tether, and dasheth thro' the plain, spurning it,
being wont to bathe himself in the fair-running river, rioting,

and reareth his head, and his mane flieth back on either
shoulder, and he glorieth in his beauty, and his knees bear
him at the gallop to the haunts and meadows of the mares ;
so ran the son of Priam, Paris, from the height of Pergamus,
all in arms, glittering like the sun, laughing for light-hearted-
ness, and his swift feet bare him.

In February 1865 Tennyson lost the mother whose
portrait he drew in *Isabel*,—"a thing enskied and
sainted."

In the autumn of 1865 the Tennysons went on a
Continental tour, and visited Waterloo, Weimar, and
Dresden; in September they entertained Emma I.,
Queen of the Sandwich Islands. The months passed
quietly at home or in town. The poet had written his
Lucretius, and, to please Sir George Grove, wrote *The
Song of the Wrens*, for music. Tennyson had not that
positive aversion to music which marked Dr Johnson,
Victor Hugo, Théophile Gautier, and some other poets.
Nay, he liked Beethoven, which places him higher
in the musical scale than Scott, who did not rise above
a Border lilt or a Jacobite ditty. The Wren songs,
entitled *The Window*, were privately printed by Sir Ivor
Guest in 1867, were set to music by Sir Arthur Sullivan,
and published by Strahan in December 1870. "A puppet," Tennyson called the song-book, " whose only merit
is, perhaps, that it can dance to Mr Sullivan's instru-
ment. I am sorry that my puppet should have to dance
at all in the dark shadow of these days" (the siege of
Paris), "but the music is now completed, and I am
bound by my promise." The verses are described as

"partly in the old style," but the true old style of the Elizabethan and cavalier days is lost.

In the summer of 1867 the Tennysons moved to a farmhouse near Haslemere, at that time not a centre of literary Londoners. "Sandy soil and heather-scented air" allured them, and the result was the purchase of land, and the building of Aldworth, Mr Knowles being the architect. In autumn Tennyson visited Lyme Regis, and, like all other travellers thither, made a pilgrimage to the Cobb, sacred to Louisa Musgrove. The poet now began the study of Hebrew, having a mind to translate the Book of Job, a vision unfulfilled. In 1868 he thought of publishing his boyish piece, *The Lover's Tale*, but delayed. An anonymously edited piracy of this and other poems was perpetrated in 1875, limited, at least nominally, to fifty copies.

In July Longfellow visited Tennyson. "The Longfellows and he talked much of spiritualism, for he was greatly interested in that subject, but he suspended his judgment, and thought that, if in such manifestations there is anything, 'Pucks, not the spirits of dead men, reveal themselves.'" This was Southey's suggestion, as regards the celebrated disturbances in the house of the Wesleys. "Wit might have much to say, wisdom, little," said Sam Wesley. Probably the talk about David Dunglas Home, the "medium" then in vogue, led to the discussion of "spiritualism." We do not hear that Tennyson ever had the curiosity to see Home, whom Mr Browning so firmly detested.

In September *The Holy Grail* was begun : it was finished "in about a week. It came like a breath of inspiration." The subject had for many years been turned about in the poet's mind, which, of course, was busy in these years of apparent inactivity. At this time (August 1868) Tennyson left his old publishers, the Moxons, for Mr Strahan, who endured till 1872. Then he was succeeded by Messrs H. S. King & Co., who gave place (1879) to Messrs Kegan Paul & Co., while in 1884 Messrs Macmillan became, and continue to be, the publishers. A few pieces, except *Lucretius* (*Macmillan's Magazine*, May 1868) unimportant, appeared in serials.

Very early in 1869 *The Coming of Arthur* was composed, while Tennyson was reading Browning's *The Ring and the Book.* He and his great contemporary were on terms of affectionate friendship, though Tennyson, perhaps, appreciated less of Browning than Browning of Tennyson. Meanwhile "Old Fitz" kept up a fire of unsympathetic growls at Browning and all his works. "I have been trying in vain to read it" (*The Ring and the Book*), "and yet the *Athenæum* tells me it is wonderfully fine." FitzGerald's ply had been taken long ago ; he wanted verbal music in poetry (no exorbitant desire), while, in Browning, *carmina desunt.* Perhaps, too, a personal feeling, as if Browning was Tennyson's rival, affected the judgment of the author of *Omar Kháyyám.* We may almost call him "the author."

The Holy Grail, with the smaller poems, such as *Lucretius*, was published at the end of 1869. Fitz-Gerald appears to have preferred *The Northern Farmer*, "the substantial rough-spun nature I knew," to all the visionary knights in the airy Quest. To compare "——" (obviously Browning) with Tennyson, was "to compare an old Jew's curiosity shop with the Phidian Marbles." Tennyson's poems "being clear to the bottom as well as beautiful, do not seem to cockney eyes so deep as muddy waters."

In November 1870 *The Last Tournament* was begun; it was finished in May 1871. Conceivably the vulgar scandals of the last days of the French Imperial *régime* may have influenced Tennyson's picture of the corruption of Arthur's Court; but the Empire did not begin, like the Round Table, with aspirations after the Ideal. In the autumn of the year Tennyson entertained, and was entertained by, Mr Huxley. In their ideas about ultimate things two men could not vary more widely, but each delighted in the other's society. In the spring of 1872 Tennyson visited Paris and the ruins of the Louvre. He read Victor Hugo, and Alfred de Musset, whose comedies he admired. The little that we hear of his opinion of the other great poet runs to this effect, "Victor Hugo is an unequal genius, sometimes sublime; he reminds one that there is but one step between the sublime and the ridiculous," but the example by which Tennyson illustrated this was derived from one of the poet's novels. In these we meet not only the sublime and the ridiculous, but passages which leave us in some perplexity as to their true category. One would have expected Hugo's lyrics to be Tennyson's favourites, but only *Gastibelza* is mentioned in that character. At this time Tennyson was vexed by

"Art with poisonous honey stolen from France,"

a phrase which cannot apply to Hugo. Meanwhile *Gareth* was being written, and the knight's song for *The Coming of Arthur*. *Gareth and Lynette*, with minor pieces, appeared in 1872. *Balin and Balan* was composed later, to lead up to *Vivien*, to which, perhaps, *Balin and Balan* was introduction sufficient had it been the earlier written. But the Idylls have already been discussed as arranged in sequence. The completion of the Idylls, with the patriotic epilogue, was followed by the offer of a baronetcy. Tennyson preferred that he and his wife "should remain plain Mr and Mrs," though "I hope that I have too much of the old-world loyalty not to wear my lady's favours against all comers, should you think that it would be more agreeable to her Majesty that I should do so."

The Idylls ended, Tennyson in 1874 began to contemplate a drama, choosing the topic, perhaps neither popular nor in an Aristotelian sense tragic, of Mary Tudor. This play was published, and put on the stage by Sir Henry Irving in 1875. *Harold* followed in 1876, *The Cup* in 1881 (at the Lyceum), *The Promise of May* (at the Globe) in 1882, *Becket* in 1884, with *The Foresters* in 1892. It seems best to consider all the dramatic period of Tennyson's work, a period reached so strangely late in his career, in the sequence of the Plays. The task is one from which I shrink, as conscious of entire ignorance of the stage and of lack of enthusiasm for the drama. Great dramatic authors have, almost invariably, had long practical knowledge of the scenes and of what is behind them. Shakespeare and his contemporaries, Molière and his contemporaries, had lived their lives on the boards and in the *foyer*, actors themselves, or in daily touch with actors and actresses. In the present day successful playwrights appear to live much in the world of the players. They have practical knowledge of the conventions and conditions which the stage imposes. Neither Browning nor Mr Swinburne (to take great names) has had, it seems, much of this practical and daily experience ; their dramas have been acted but rarely, if at all, and many examples prove that neither poetical genius nor the genius for prose fiction can enable men to produce plays which hold their own on the boards. This may be the fault of public taste, or partly of public taste, partly of defect in practical knowledge on the side of the authors. Of the stage, by way of practice, Tennyson had known next to nothing, yet his dramas were written to be acted, and acted some of them were. "For himself, he was aware," says his biographer, "that he wanted intimate knowledge of the mechanical

details necessary for the modern stage, although in
early and middle life he had been a constant play-
goer, and would keenly follow the action of a play,
criticising the characterisation, incidents, scenic effects,
situations, language, and dramatic points." He was
quite prepared to be "edited" for acting purposes by
the players. Miss Mary Anderson says that "he was
ready to sacrifice even his *most* beautiful lines for the
sake of a real dramatic effect."

This proved unusual common - sense in a poet.
Modern times and manners are notoriously unfavourable
to the serious drama. In the age of the Greek tra-
gedians, as in the days of "Eliza and our James,"
reading was not very common, and life was much more
passed in public than among ourselves, when people go
to the play for light recreation, or to be shocked. So
various was the genius of Tennyson, that had he devoted
himself early to the stage, and had he been backed by a
manager with the enterprise and intelligence of Sir
Henry Irving, it is impossible to say how much he
might have done to restore the serious drama. But we
cannot regret that he was occupied in his prime with
other things, nor can we expect to find his noblest and
most enduring work in the dramatic experiments of his
latest years. It is notable that, in his opinion, "the
conditions of the dramatic art are much more complex
than they were." For example, we have "the star
system," which tends to allot what is, or was, technically
styled "the fat," to one or two popular players. Now,

a poet like Tennyson will inevitably distribute large quantities of what is most excellent to many characters, and the consequent difficulties may be appreciated by students of our fallen nature. The poet added that to be a first-rate historical playwright means much more work than formerly, seeing that " exact history " has taken the part of the chance chronicle."

This is a misfortune. The dramas of the Attic stage, with one or two exceptions, are based on myth and legend, not on history, and even in the *Persæ*, grounded on contemporary events, Æschylus introduced the ghost of Darius, not vouched for by " exact history." Let us conceive Shakespeare writing *Macbeth* in an age of " exact history." Hardly any of the play would be left. Fleance and Banquo must go. Duncan becomes a young man, and far from " gracious." Macbeth appears as the defender of the legitimist prince, Lulach, against Duncan, a usurper. Lady Macbeth is a pattern to her sex, and her lord is a clement and sagacious ruler. The witches are ruled out of the piece. Difficulties arise about the English aid to Malcolm. History, in fact, declines to be dramatic. Liberties must be taken. In his plays of the Mary Stuart cycle, Mr Swinburne telescopes the affair of Darnley into that of Chastelard, which was much earlier. He makes Mary Beaton (in love with Chastelard) a kind of avenging fate, who will never leave the Queen till her head falls at Fotheringay; though, in fact, after a flirtation with Randolph, Mary Beaton married Ogilvy of Boyne (really in love with

Lady Bothwell), and not one of the four Maries was at Fotheringay. An artist ought to be allowed to follow legend, of its essence dramatic, or to manipulate history as he pleases. Our modern scrupulosity is pedantic. But Tennyson read a long list of books for his *Queen Mary*, though it does not appear that he made original researches in MSS. These labours occupied 1874 and 1875. Yet it would be foolish to criticise his *Queen Mary* as if we were criticising " exact history." " The play's the thing."

The poet thought that " Bloody Mary" " had been harshly judged by the verdict of popular tradition." So have most characters to whom popular dislike affixes the popular epithet — " Bloody Claverse," " Bloody Mackenzie," " Bloody Balfour." Mary had the courage of the Tudors. She "edified all around her by her cheerfulness, her piety, and her resignation to the will of Providence," in her last days (Lingard). Camden calls her "a queen never praised enough for the purity of her morals, her charity to the poor" (she practised as a district visitor), "and her liberality to the nobles and the clergy." She was " pious, merciful, pure, and ever to be praised, if we overlook her erroneous opinions in religion," says Godwin. She had been grievously wronged from her youth upwards. In Elizabeth she had a sister and a rival, a constant intriguer against her, and a kinswoman far from amiable. Despite " the kindness and attention of Philip " (Lingard), affairs of State demanded his absence from England. The disappoint-

ment as to her expected child was cruel. She knew
that she had become unpopular, and she could not
look for the success of her Church, to which she was sin-
cerely attached.   M. Auguste Filon thought that *Queen
Mary* might secure dramatic rank for Tennyson, "if a
great actress arose who conceived a passion for the part
of Mary." But that was not to be expected. Mary
was middle-aged, plain, and in aspect now terrible, now
rueful. No great actress will throw herself with passion
into such an ungrateful part.   "Throughout all history,"
Tennyson said, "there was nothing more mournful than
the final tragedy of this woman." *Mournful* it is, but
not tragic. There is nothing grand at the close, as
when Mary Stuart conquers death and evil fame, redeeming herself by her courage and her calm, and extending
over unborn generations that witchery which her enemies
dreaded more than an army with banners.

Moreover, popular tradition can never forgive the fires
of Smithfield. It was Mary Tudor's misfortune that she
had the power to execute, on a great scale, that faculty
of persecution to the death for which her Presbyterian
and other Protestant opponents pined in vain.   Mr
Froude says of her, " For the first and last time the
true Ultramontane spirit was dominant in England, the
genuine conviction that, as the orthodox prophets and
sovereigns of Israel slew the worshippers of Baal, so
were Catholic rulers called upon, as their first duty,
to extirpate heretics as the enemies of God and

man." That was precisely the spirit of Knox and
other Presbyterian denouncers of death against " Idola-
ters " (Catholics). But the Scottish preachers were
always thwarted : Mary and her advisers had their way,
as, earlier, Latimer had preached against sufferers at
the stake. To the stake, which he feared so greatly,
Cranmer had sent persons not of his own fleeting shade
of theological opinion. These men had burned Ana-
baptists, but all that is lightly forgotten by Protestant
opinion. Under Mary (whoever may have been
primarily responsible) Cranmer and Latimer were treated
as they had treated others. Moreover, some two hundred
poor men and women had dared the fiery death. The
persecution was on a scale never forgiven or forgotten,
since Mary began *cerdonibus esse timenda*. Mary was
not essentially inclement. Despite Renard, the agent
of the Emperor, she spared that lord of fluff and feather,
Courtenay, and she spared Elizabeth. Lady Jane she
could not save, the girl who was a queen by grace of
God and of her own royal nature. But Mary will never
be pardoned by England. " Few men or women have
lived less capable of doing knowingly a wrong thing,"
says Mr Froude, a great admirer of Tennyson's play.
Yet, taking Mr Froude's own view, Mary's abject and
superannuated passion for Philip ; her ecstasies during
her supposed pregnancy ; " the forlorn hours when she
would sit on the ground with her knees drawn to her
face," with all her " symptoms of hysterical derangement,

leave little room, as we think of her, for other feelings than pity." Unfortunately, feelings of pity for a person so distraught, so sourly treated by fortune, do not suffice for tragedy. When we contemplate Antigone or Œdipus, it is not with a sentiment of pity struggling against abhorrence.

For these reasons the play does not seem to have a good dramatic subject. The unity is given by Mary herself and her fortunes, and these are scarcely dramatic. History prevents the introduction of Philip till the second scene of the third act. His entrance is *manqué;* he merely accompanies Cardinal Pole, who takes command of the scene, and Philip does not get in a word till after a long conversation between the Queen and the Cardinal. Previously Philip had only crossed the stage in a procession, yet when he does appear he is bereft of prominence. The interest as regards him is indicated, in Act I. scene v., by Mary's kissing his miniature. Her blighted love for him is one main motive of the tragedy, but his own part appears too subordinate in the play as published. The interest is scattered among the vast crowd of characters; and Mr R. H. Hutton remarked at the time that he "remains something of a cold, cruel, and sensual shadow." We are more interested in Wyatt, Cranmer, Gardiner, and others; or at least their parts are more interesting. Yet in no case does the interest of any character, except of Mary and Elizabeth, remain continuous throughout the play. Tennyson himself thought that "the real difficulty of the drama is to give sufficient relief to its intense sadness. . . . Nothing less than the holy calm of the meek and penitent Cranmer can be adequate artistic relief." But not much relief can be drawn from a man about to be burned alive, and history does not tempt us to keen sympathy with the recanting archbishop, at least if we agree with Macaulay rather than with Froude.

I venture to think that historical tradition, as usual, offered a better motive than exact history. Following tradition, we see in Mary a cloud of hateful gloom, from which England escapes into the glorious dawn of "the Gospel light," and of Elizabeth, who might be made a triumphantly sympathetic character. That is the natural and popular course which the drama might take. But Tennyson's history is almost critical and scientific. Points of difficult and debated evidence (as to Elizabeth's part in Wyatt's rebellion) are discussed. There is no contest of day and darkness, of Truth and Error. The characters are in that perplexed condition about creeds which was their actual state after the political and social and religious chaos produced by Henry VIII. Gardiner is a Catholic, but not an Ultramontane; Lord William Howard is a Catholic, but not a fanatic; we find a truculent Anabaptist, or Socialist, and a citizen whose pride is his moderation. The native uncritical tendency of the

M

drama is to throw up hats and halloo for Elizabeth and an open Bible.   In place of this, Cecil delivers a well-considered analysis of the character of Elizabeth :—

> " *Eliz.*   God guide me lest I lose the way.
>   [*Exit* Elizabeth.
> *Cecil.* Many points weather'd, many perilous ones,
> At last a harbour opens ; but therein
> Sunk rocks—they need fine steering—much it is
> To be nor mad, nor bigot—have a mind—
> Nor let Priests' talk, or dream of worlds to be,
> Miscolour things about her—sudden touches
> For him, or him—sunk rocks ; no passionate faith—
> But—if let be—balance and compromise ;
> Brave, wary, sane to the heart of her—a Tudor
> School'd by the shadow of death—a Boleyn, too,
> Glancing across the Tudor—not so well."

This is excellent as historical criticism, in the favourable sense ; but the drama, by its nature, demands something not critical but triumphant and one-sided.   The character of Elizabeth is one of the best in the play, as her soliloquy (Act III. scene v.) is one of the finest of the speeches.   We see her courage, her coquetry, her dissimulation, her arrogance.   But while this is the true Elizabeth, it is not the idealised Elizabeth whom English loyalty created, lived for, and died for.   Mr Froude wrote, "You have given us the greatest of all your works," an opinion which the world can never accept.   "You have reclaimed one more section of English History from the wilderness, and given it a form in which it will be fixed for ever.   No one since Shakespeare has done that."   But Mr Froude had done it, and

Tennyson's reading of "the section" is mainly that of
Mr Froude.   Mr Gladstone found that Cranmer and
Gardiner "are still in a considerable degree mysteries
to me."   A mystery Cranmer must remain.   Perhaps
the "crowds" and "Voices" are not the least excellent
of the characters, Tennyson's humour finding an opportunity in them, and in Joan and Tib.   His idyllic
charm speaks in the words of Lady Clarence to the
fevered Queen ; and there is dramatic genius in her
reply :—

> "*Mary*. What is the strange thing happiness?   Sit down
>   here :
> Tell me thine happiest hour.
>   *Lady Clarence*.   I will, if that
> May make your Grace forget yourself a little.
> There runs a shallow brook across our field
> For twenty miles, where the black crow flies five,
> And doth so bound and babble all the way
> As if itself were happy.   It was May-time,
> And I was walking with the man I loved.
> I loved him, but I thought I was not loved.
> And both were silent, letting the wild brook
> Speak for us—till he stoop'd and gather'd one
> From out a bed of thick forget-me-nots,
> Look'd hard and sweet at me, and gave it me.
> I took it, tho' I did not know I took it,
> And put it in my bosom, and all at once
> I felt his arms about me, and his lips——
>   *Mary*. O God! I have been too slack, too slack;
> There are Hot Gospellers even among our guards—
> Nobles we dared not touch.   We have but burnt
> The heretic priest, workmen, and women and children.
> Wet, famine, ague, fever, storm, wreck, wrath,—

We have so play'd the coward ; but by God's grace,
We'll follow Philip's leading, and set up
The Holy Office here—garner the wheat,
And burn the tares with unquenchable fire !"

The conclusion, in the acting edition, printed in the
Biography, appears to be an improvement on that in the
text as originally published. Unhappy as the drama
essentially is, the welcome which Mr Browning gave both
to the published work and to the acted play—" a complete success " : " conception, execution, the whole and
the parts, I see nowhere the shadow of a fault "—offers
" relief" in actual human nature. " He is the greatest-
brained poet in England," Tennyson said, on a later
occasion. " Violets fade, he has given me a crown of
gold."

Before writing _Harold_ (1876) the poet " studied
many recent plays," and re-read Æschylus and
Sophocles. For history he went to the Bayeux
tapestry, the _Roman de Rou_, Lord Lytton, and Freeman.
Students of a recent controversy will observe that,
following Freeman, he retains the famous palisade, so
grievously battered by the axe-strokes of Mr Horace
Round. _Harold_ is a piece more compressed, and much
more in accordance with the traditions of the drama,
than _Queen Mary_. The topic is tragic indeed : the
sorrow being that of a great man, a great king, the bul-
wark of a people that fell with his fall. Moreover, as the
topic is treated, the play is rich in the irony usually asso-
ciated with the name of Sophocles. Victory comes

before a fall.   Harold, like Antigone, is torn between two
duties—his oath and the claims of his country.   His
ruin comes from what Aristotle would call his ἁμαρτία,
his fault in swearing the oath to William.   The hero
himself, recking little, after a superstitious moment, of
the concealed relics over which he swore, deems his
offence to lie in swearing a vow which he never meant
to keep.   The persuasions which urge him to this
course are admirably presented : England, Edith, his
brother's freedom, were at stake.   Casuistry, or even
law, would have absolved him easily ; an oath taken
under duresse is of no avail.   But Harold's " honour
rooted in dishonour stood," and he cannot so readily
absolve himself.   Bruce and the bishops who stood by
Bruce had no such scruples : they perjured themselves
often, on the most sacred relics, especially the bishops.
But Harold rises above the mediæval and magical conception of the oath, and goes to his doom conscious of
a stain on his honour, of which only a deeper stain,
that of falseness to his country, could make him clean.
This is a truly tragic stroke of destiny.   The hero's
character is admirably noble, patient, and simple.   The
Confessor also is as true in art as to history, and his
vision of the fall and rise of England is a noble passage.
In Aldwyth we have something of Vivien, with a grain
of conscience, and the part of Edith Swan's-neck has
a restrained and classic pathos in contrast with the
melancholy of Wulfnoth.   The piece, as the poet said,
is a "tragedy of doom," of deepening and darkening

omens, as in the *Odyssey* and *Njal's Saga.* The battle
scene, with the choruses of the monks, makes a noble
close.

FitzGerald remained loyal, but it was to "a fairy
Prince who came from other skies than these rainy
ones," and "the wretched critics," as G. H. Lewes
called them, seem to have been unfriendly. In fact
(besides the innate wretchedness of all critics), they
grudged the time and labour given to the drama, in
an undramatic age. *Harold* had not what FitzGerald
called "the old champagne flavour" of the vintage
of 1842.

Becket was begun in 1876, printed in 1879, and
published in 1884. Before that date, in 1880, Tennyson produced one of the volumes of poetry which was
more welcome than a play to most of his admirers.
The intervening years passed in the Isle of Wight, at
Aldworth, in town, and in summer tours, were of no
marked biographical interest. The poet was close on
three score and ten—he reached that limit in 1879.
The days darkened around him, as darken they must:
in the spring of 1879 he lost his favourite brother,
himself a poet of original genius, Charles Tennyson
Turner. In May of the same year he published *The
Lover's Tale,* which has been treated here among his
earliest works. His hours, and (to some extent) his
meals, were regulated by Sir Andrew Clark. He
planted trees, walked, read, loitered in his garden, and
kept up his old friendships, while he made that of the

great Gordon. Compliments passed between him and Victor Hugo, who had entertained Lionel Tennyson in Paris, and wrote: "Je lis avec émotion vos vers superbes ; c'est un reflet de gloire que vous m'envoyez." Mr Matthew Arnold's compliment was very like Mr Arnold's humour: "Your father has been our most popular poet for over forty years, and I am of opinion that he fully deserves his reputation": such was "Mat's sublime waggery." Tennyson heaped coals of fire on the other poet, bidding him, as he liked to be bidden, to write more poetry, not "prose things." Tennyson lived much in the society of Browning and George Eliot, and made the acquaintance of Renan. In December 1879 Mr and Mrs Kendal produced *The Falcon*, which ran for sixty-seven nights; it is "an exquisite little poem in action," as Fanny Kemble said. During a Continental tour Tennyson visited Catullus's Sirmio: "here he made his *Frater Ave atque Vale;*" and the poet composed his beautiful salutation to the

"Tenderest of Roman poets nineteen hundred years ago."

In 1880 *Ballads and other Poems* proved that, like Titian, the great poet was not to be defeated by the years. *The First Quarrel* was in his most popular English style. *Rizpah* deserved and received the splendid panegyric of Mr Swinburne. *The Revenge* is probably the finest of the patriotic pieces, and keeps green the memory of an exploit the most marvellous in the annals of English seamen. *The Village Wife* is a pendant worthy of

The Northern Farmer. The poem *In the Children's Hospital* caused some irritation at the moment, but there was only one opinion as to the *Defence of Lucknow* and the beautiful re-telling of the Celtic *Voyage of Maeldune.* The fragment of Homeric translation was equally fortunate in choice of subject and in rendering.

In the end of 1880 the poet finished *The Cup*, which had been worked on occasionally since he completed *The Falcon* in 1880. The piece was read by the author to Sir Henry Irving and his company, and it was found that the manuscript copy needed few alterations to fit it for the stage. The scenery and the acting of the protagonists are not easily to be forgotten. The play ran for a hundred and thirty nights. Sir Henry Irving had thought that *Becket* (then unpublished) would prove too expensive, and could only be a *succès d'estime.* Tennyson had found out that "the worst of writing for the stage is, you must keep some actor always in your mind." To this necessity authors like Molière and Shakespeare were, of course, resigned and familiar; they knew exactly how to deal with all their means. But this part of the business of play-writing must always be a cross to the poet who is not at one with the world of the stage.

In *The Cup* Miss Ellen Terry made the strongest impression, her part being noble and sympathetic, while Sir Henry Irving had the ungrateful part of the villain. To be sure, he was a villain of much complexity; and Tennyson thought that his subtle blend of Roman refinement and intellectuality, and barbarian, self-satisfied sensuality, was not "hit off." Synorix is, in fact, half-Greek, half-Celt, with a Roman education, and the "blend" is rather too remote for successful representation. The traditional villain, from Iago downwards, is not apt to utter such poetry as this :—

> "O Thou, that dost inspire the germ with life,
> The child, a thread within the house of birth,
> And give him limbs, then air, and send him forth
> The glory of his father—Thou whose breath
> Is balmy wind to robe our hills with grass,
> And kindle all our vales with myrtle-blossom,
> And roll the golden oceans of our grain,
> And sway the long grape-bunches of our vines,
> And fill all hearts with fatness and the lust
> Of plenty—make me happy in my marriage !"

The year 1881 brought the death of another of the old Cambridge friends, James Spedding, the biographer of Bacon ; and Carlyle also died, a true friend, if rather intermittent in his appreciation of poetry. The real Carlyle did appreciate it, but the Carlyle of attitude was too much of the iron Covenanter to express what he felt. The poem *Despair* irritated the earnest and serious readers of "know-nothing books." The poem expressed, dramatically, a mood like another, a human mood not so very uncommon. A man ruined in this world's happiness curses the faith of his youth, and the unfaith of his reading and reflection, and tries to drown himself. This is one conclusion of the practical syllogism, and it is a free country. However, there were freethinkers who did not think that Tennyson's kind of thinking ought to be free. Other earnest persons objected to "First drink a health," in the re-fashioned song of *Hands all Round.* They might have remembered a royal health drunk in water an hour before the drinkers swept Mackay down the Pass of Killiecrankie. The poet did not specify the fluid in which the toast was to be carried, and the cup might be that which "cheers but not inebriates." "The common cup," as the remonstrants had to be informed, "has in all ages been the sacred symbol of unity."

The Promise of May was produced in November 1882, and the poet was once more so unfortunate as to vex the susceptibilities of advanced thinkers. The play is not a masterpiece, and yet neither the gallery gods nor the Marquis of Queensberry need have felt their withers wrung. The hero, or villain, Edgar, is a perfectly impossible person, and represents no kind of political, social, or economical thinker. A man would give all other bliss and all his worldly wealth for this, to waste his whole strength in one kick upon this perfect prig. He employs the arguments of evolution and so forth to justify the seduction of a little girl of fifteen, and later, by way of making amends, proposes to commit incest by marrying her sister. There have been evolutionists, to be sure, who believed in promiscuity, like Mr Edgar, as preferable to monogamy. But this only proves that an evolutionist may fail to understand evolution. There be also such folk as Stevenson calls " squir-

radicals" — squires who say that "the land is the
people's." Probably no advocate of promiscuity, and
no squirradical, was present at the performances of
The Promise of May. But people of advanced minds
had got it into their heads that their doctrines were to be
attacked, so they went and made a hubbub in the sacred
cause of freedom of thought and speech. The truth is,
that controversial topics, political topics, ought not to be
brought into plays, much less into sermons. Tennyson
meant Edgar for "nothing thorough, nothing sincere."
He is that venomous thing, the prig-scoundrel : he does
not suit the stage, and his place, if anywhere, is in the
novel. Advocates of marriage with a deceased wife's
sister might have applauded Edgar for wishing to marry
the sister of a mistress assumed to be deceased, but no
other party in the State wanted anything except the
punching of Edgar's head by Farmer Dobson.

In 1883 died Edward FitzGerald, the most kind,
loyal, and, as he said, crotchety of old and dear Cambridge friends. He did not live to see the delightful
poem which Tennyson had written for him. In almost
his latest letter he had remarked, superfluously, that
when he called the task of translating *The Agamemnon*
"work for a poet," he "was not thinking of Mr
Browning."

In the autumn of 1883 Tennyson was taken, with Mr
Gladstone, by Sir Donald Currie, for a cruise round the
west coast of Scotland, to the Orkneys, and to Copenhagen. The people of Kirkwall conferred on the poet

and the statesman the freedom of the burgh, and Mr Gladstone, in an interesting speech, compared the relative chances of posthumous fame of the poet and the politician. Pericles is not less remembered than Sophocles, though Shakespeare is more in men's minds than Cecil. Much depends, as far as the statesmen are considered, on contemporary historians. It is Thucydides who immortalises Pericles. But it is improbable that the things which Mr Gladstone did, and attempted, will be forgotten more rapidly than the conduct and characters of, say, Burleigh or Lethington.

In 1884, after this voyage, with its royal functions and celebrations at Copenhagen, a peerage was offered to the poet. He " did not want to alter his plain Mr," and he must have known that, whether he accepted or refused, the chorus of blame would be louder than that of applause. Scott had desired " such grinning honour as Sir Walter hath " ; the title went well with the old name, and pleased his love of old times. Tennyson had been blamed " by literary men " for thrice evading a baronetcy, and he did not think that a peerage would make smooth the lives of his descendants. But he concluded, " Why should I be selfish and not suffer an honour (as Gladstone says) to be done to literature in my name ? " Politically, he thought that the Upper House, while it lasts, partly supplied the place of the American " referendum." He voted in July 1884 for the extension of the franchise, and in November stated his views to Mr Gladstone in verse. In prose he wrote to Mr

Gladstone, "I have a strong conviction that the more simple the dealings of men with men, as well as of man with man, are—the better," a sentiment which, perhaps, did not always prevail with his friend. The poet's reflections on the horror of Gordon's death are not recorded. He introduced the idea of the Gordon Home for Boys, and later supported it by a letter, "Have we forgotten Gordon?" to the *Daily Telegraph*. They who cannot forget Gordon must always be grateful to Tennyson for providing this opportunity of honouring the greatest of an illustrious clan, and of helping, in their degree, a scheme which was dear to the heroic leader. The poet, very naturally, was most averse to personal appearance in public matters. Mankind is so fashioned that the advice of a poet is always regarded as unpractical, and is even apt to injure the cause which he advocates. Happily there cannot be two opinions about the right way of honouring Gordon. Tennyson's poem, *The Fleet*, was also in harmony with the general sentiment.

In the last month of 1884 *Becket* was published. The theme of Fair Rosamund had appealed to the poet in youth, and he had written part of a lyric which he judiciously left unpublished. It is given in his Biography. In 1877 he had visited Canterbury, and had traced the steps of Becket to his place of slaughter in the Cathedral. The poem was printed in 1879, but not published till seven years later. In 1879 Sir Henry Irving had thought the play too costly to be produced with

more than a *succès d'estime ;* but in 1891 he put it on the
stage, where it proved the most successful of modern
poetic dramas.   As published it is, obviously, far too
long for public performance.   It is not easy to understand why dramatic poets always make their works so
much too long.   The drama seems, by its very nature,
to have a limit almost as distinct as the limit of the
sonnet.   It is easy to calculate how long a play for the
stage ought to be, and we might think that a poet would
find the natural limit serviceable to his art, for it
inculcates selection, conciseness, and concentration.
But despite these advantages of the natural form of the
drama, modern poets, at least, constantly overflow their
banks.   The author *ruit profusus*, and the manager has
to reduce the piece to feasible proportions, such as it
ought to have assumed from the first.

Becket has been highly praised by Sir Henry Irving
himself, for its " moments of passion and pathos, . . .
which, when they exist, atone to an audience for the
endurance of long acts."   But why should the audience
have such long acts to endure ?   The reader, one fears,
is apt to use his privilege of skipping.   The long
speeches of Walter Map and the immense period of
Margery tempt the student to exercise his agility.   A
" chronicle play " has the privilege of wandering, but
Becket wanders too far and too long.   The political
details of the quarrel between Church and State, with
its domestic and international complexities, are apt to
fatigue the attention.   Inevitable and insoluble as the

situation was, neither protagonist is entirely sympathetic,
whether in the play or in history. The struggle in
Becket between his love of the king and his duty to the
Church (or what he takes to be his duty) is nobly presented, and is truly dramatic, while there is grotesque
and terrible relief in the banquet of the Beggars. In
the scene of the assassination the poet "never stoops
his wing," and there are passages of tender pathos
between Henry and Rosamund, while Becket's keen
memories of his early days, just before his death,
are moving.

> "*Becket.* I once was out with Henry in the days
> When Henry loved me, and we came upon
> A wild-fowl sitting on her nest, so still
> I reach'd my hand and touch'd ; she did not stir ;
> The snow had frozen round her, and she sat
> Stone-dead upon a heap of ice-cold eggs.
> Look ! how this love, this mother, runs thro' all
> The world God made—even the beast—the bird !
>   *John of Salisbury.* Ay, still a lover of the beast and
>   bird?
> But these arm'd men—will you not hide yourself?
> Perchance the fierce De Brocs from Saltwood Castle,
> To assail our Holy Mother lest she brood
> Too long o'er this hard egg, the world, and send
> Her whole heart's heat into it, till it break
> Into young angels. Pray you, hide yourself.
>   *Becket.* There was a little fair-hair'd Norman maid
> Lived in my mother's house : if Rosamund is
> The world's rose, as her name imports her—she
> Was the world's lily.
>   *John of Salisbury.* Ay, and what of her?
>   *Becket.* She died of leprosy."

But the part of Rosamund, her innocent ignorance especially, is not very readily intelligible, not quite persuasive, and there is almost a touch of the burlesque in her unexpected appearance as a monk. To weave that old and famous story of love into the terribly complex political intrigue was a task almost too great. The character of Eleanor is perhaps more successfully drawn in the Prologue than in the scene where she offers the choice of the dagger or the bowl, and is interrupted, in a startlingly unexpected manner, by the Archbishop himself. The opportunities for scenic effects are magnificent throughout, and must have contributed greatly to the success on the stage. Still one cannot but regard the published *Becket* as rather the marble from which the statue may be hewn than as the statue itself. There are fine scenes, powerful and masterly drawing of character in Henry, Eleanor, and Becket, but there is a want of concentration, due, perhaps, to the long period of time covered by the action. So, at least, it seems to a reader who has admitted his sense of incompetency in the dramatic region. The acuteness of the poet's power of historical intuition was attested by Mr J. R. Green and Mr Bryce. "One cannot imagine," said Mr Bryce, "a more vivid, a more perfectly faithful picture than it gives both of Henry and Thomas." Tennyson's portraits of these two "go beyond and perfect history." The poet's sympathy ought, perhaps, to have been, if not with the false and ruffianly Henry, at least

with Henry's side of the question.   For Tennyson had
made Harold leave

"To England
My legacy of war against the Pope
From child to child, from Pope to Pope, from age to age,
Till the sea wash her level with her shores,
Or till the Pope be Christ's."

N

IX.

LAST YEARS.

THE end of 1884 saw the publication of *Tiresias and other Poems*, dedicated to "My good friend, Robert Browning," and opening with the beautiful verses to one who never was Mr Browning's friend, Edward Fitz-Gerald. The volume is rich in the best examples of Tennyson's later work. *Tiresias*, the monologue of the aged seer, blinded by excess of light when he beheld Athene unveiled, and under the curse of Cassandra, is worthy of the author who, in youth, wrote *Œnone* and *Ulysses*. Possibly the verses reflect Tennyson's own sense of public indifference to the voice of the poet and the seer. But they are of much earlier date than the year of publication :—

> " For when the crowd would roar
> For blood, for war, whose issue was their doom,
> To cast wise words among the multitude
> Was flinging fruit to lions ; nor, in hours
> Of civil outbreak, when I knew the twain
> Would each waste each, and bring on both the yoke
> Of stronger states, was mine the voice to curb
> The madness of our cities and their kings.

Who ever turn'd upon his heel to hear
My warning that the tyranny of one
Was prelude to the tyranny of all?
My counsel that the tyranny of all
Led backward to the tyranny of one?
    This power hath work'd no good to aught that lives."

The conclusion was a favourite with the author, and his
blank verse never reached a higher strain :—

                    " But for me,
I would that I were gather'd to my rest,
And mingled with the famous kings of old,
On whom about their ocean-islets flash
The faces of the Gods—the wise man's word,
Here trampled by the populace underfoot,
There crown'd with worship—and these eyes will find
The men I knew, and watch the chariot whirl
About the goal again, and hunters race
The shadowy lion, and the warrior-kings,
In height and prowess more than human, strive
Again for glory, while the golden lyre
Is ever sounding in heroic ears
Heroic hymns, and every way the vales
Wind, clouded with the grateful incense-fume
Of those who mix all odour to the Gods
On one far height in one far-shining fire."

Then follows the pathetic piece on FitzGerald's death,
and the prayer, not unfulfilled—

                " That, when I from hence
Shall fade with him into the unknown,
    My close of earth's experience
    May prove as peaceful as his own."

The Ancient Sage, with its lyric interludes, is one of
Tennyson's meditations on the mystery of the world and

of existence.   Like the poet himself, the Sage finds a
gleam of light and hope in his own subjective experiences
of some unspeakable condition, already recorded in *In
Memoriam.*   The topic was one on which he seems to
have spoken to his friends with freedom :—

> "And more, my son ! for more than once when I
> Sat all alone, revolving in myself
> The word that is the symbol of myself,
> The mortal limit of the Self was loosed,
> And past into the Nameless, as a cloud
> Melts into Heaven.   I touch'd my limbs, the limbs
> Were strange not mine—and yet no shade of doubt,
> But utter clearness, and thro' loss of Self
> The gain of such large life as match'd with ours
> Were Sun to spark—unshadowable in words,
> Themselves but shadows of a shadow-world."

The poet's habit of

> " Revolving in myself
> The word that is the symbol of myself "—

that is, of dwelling on the sound of his own name,
was familiar to the Arabs.   M. Lefébure has drawn
my attention to a passage in the works of a mediæval Arab philosopher, Ibn Khaldoun :[1] "To arrive
at the highest degree of inspiration of which he is
capable, the diviner should have recourse to the use
of certain phrases marked by a peculiar cadence
and parallelism.   Thus he emancipates his mind from
the influence of the senses, and is enabled to attain
an imperfect contact with the spiritual world."   Ibn

[1] *Notices et Extraits des MSS. de la Bibliothèque Impériale,*
I. xix. pp. 643-645.

Khaldoun regards the "contact" as extremely "imperfect." He describes similar efforts made by concentrating the gaze on a mirror, a bowl of water, or the like. Tennyson was doubtless unaware that he had stumbled accidentally on a method of "ancient sages." Psychologists will explain his experience by the word "dissociation." It is not everybody, however, who can thus dissociate himself. The temperament of genius has often been subject to such influence, as M. Lefébure has shown in the modern instances of George Sand and Alfred de Musset: we might add Shelley, Goethe, and even Scott.

The poet's versatility was displayed in the appearance with these records of "weird seizures," of the Irish dialect piece *To-morrow*, the popular *Spinster's Sweet-Arts*, and the *Locksley Hall Sixty Years After*. The old fire of the versification is unabated, but the hero has relapsed on the gloom of the hero of *Maud*. He represents himself, of course, not Tennyson, or only one of the moods of Tennyson, which were sometimes black enough. A very different mood chants the *Charge of the Heavy Brigade*, and speaks of

> "Green Sussex fading into blue
> With one gray glimpse of sea."

The lines *To Virgil* were written at the request of the Mantuans, by the most Virgilian of all the successors of the

> "Wielder of the stateliest measure
> ever moulded by the lips of man."

Never was Tennyson more Virgilian than in this unmatched panegyric, the sum and flower of criticism of
that

> "Golden branch amid the shadows,
>   kings and realms that pass to rise no more."

Hardly less admirable is the tribute to Catullus, and
the old poet is young again in the bird-song of *Early
Spring*.   The lines on *Poets and their Bibliographies*, with
The Dead Prophet, express Tennyson's lifelong abhorrence of the critics and biographers, whose joy is in the
futile and the unimportant, in personal gossip and the
sweepings of the studio, the salvage of the waste-
paper basket.   The *Prefatory Poem to my Brother's
Sonnets* is not only touching in itself, but proves that
the poet can "turn to favour and to prettiness" such
an affliction as the ruinous summer of 1879.

The year 1880 brought deeper distress in the death
of the poet's son Lionel, whose illness, begun in India,
ended fatally in the Red Sea.   The interest of the following years was mainly domestic.   The poet's health,
hitherto robust, was somewhat impaired in 1888, but
his vivid interest in affairs and in letters was unabated.
He consoled himself with Virgil, Keats, Wordsworth,
Gibbon, Euripides, and Mr Leaf's speculations on the
composite nature of the *Iliad*, in which Coleridge, perhaps alone among poets, believed.   "You know," said
Tennyson to Mr Leaf, "I never liked that theory of
yours about the many poets."   It would be at least as
easy to prove that there were many authors of *Ivanhoe*,

or perhaps it would be a good deal more easy. However, he admitted that three lines which occur both in the Eighth and the Sixteenth Books of the *Iliad* are more appropriate in the later book. Similar examples might be found in his own poems. He still wrote, in the intervals of a malady which brought him "as near death as a man could be without dying." He was an example of the great physical strength which, on the whole, seems usually to accompany great mental power. The strength may be dissipated by passion, or by undue labour, as in cases easily recalled to memory, but neither cause had impaired the vigour of Tennyson. Like Goethe, he lived out all his life ; and his eightieth birthday was cheered both by public and private expressions of reverence and affection.

Of Tennyson's last three years on earth we may think, in his own words, that his

> " Life's latest eve endured
> Nor settled into hueless grey."

Nature was as dear to him and as inspiring as of old ; men and affairs and letters were not slurred by his intact and energetic mind. His *Demeter and other Poems*, with the dedication to Lord Dufferin, appeared in the December of the year. The dedication was the lament for the dead son and the salutation to the Viceroy of India, a piece of resigned and manly regret. The *Demeter and Persephone* is a modern and tender study of the theme of the most beautiful Homeric

Hymn.   The ancient poet had no such thought of the restored Persephone as that which impels Tennyson to describe her

> " Faint as a climate-changing bird that flies
>   All night across the darkness, and at dawn
>   Falls on the threshold of her native land."

The spring, the restored Persephone, comes more vigorous and joyous to the shores of the Ægean than to ours.   All Tennyson's own is Demeter's awe of those "imperial disimpassioned eyes" of her daughter, come from the bed and the throne of Hades, the Lord of many guests.   The hymn, happy in its ending, has no thought of the grey heads of the Fates, and their answer to the goddess concerning "fate beyond the Fates," and the breaking of the bonds of Hades.   The ballad of *Owd Roä* is one of the most spirited of the essays in dialect to which Tennyson had of late years inclined.   *Vastness* merely expresses, in terms of poetry, Tennyson's conviction that, without immortality, life is a series of worthless contrasts.   An opposite opinion may be entertained, but a man has a right to express his own, which, coming from so great a mind, is not undeserving of attention ; or, at least, is hardly deserving of reproof.   The poet's idea is also stated thus in *The Ring*, in terms which perhaps do not fall below the poetical ; or, at least, do not drop into "the utterly unpoetical " :—

> "The Ghost in Man, the Ghost that once was Man,
>   But cannot wholly free itself from Man,

> Are calling to each other thro' a dawn
> Stranger than earth has ever seen ; the veil
> Is rending, and the Voices of the day
> Are heard across the Voices of the dark.
> No sudden heaven, nor sudden hell, for man,
> But thro' the Will of One who knows and rules—
> And utter knowledge is but utter love—
> Æonian Evolution, swift or slow,
> Thro' all the Spheres— an ever opening height,
> An ever lessening earth."

The Ring is, in fact, a ghost story based on a legend told by Mr Lowell about a house near where he had once lived ; one of those houses vexed by

> " A footstep, a low throbbing in the walls,
> A noise of falling weights that never fell,
> Weird whispers, bells that rang without a hand,
> Door-handles turn'd when none was at the door,
> And bolted doors that open'd of themselves."

These phenomena were doubtless caused by rats and water-pipes, but they do not destroy the pity and the passion of the tale. The lines to Mary Boyle are all of the normal world, and worthy of a poet's youth and of the spring. *Merlin and the Gleam* is the spiritual allegory of the poet's own career :—

> " Arthur had vanish'd
> I knew not whither,
> The king who loved me,
> And cannot die."

So at last

> " All but in Heaven
> Hovers The Gleam,"

whither the wayfarer was soon to follow. There is a
marvellous hope and pathos in the melancholy of these
all but the latest songs, reminiscent of youth and love,
and even of the dim haunting memories and dreams of
infancy. No other English poet has thus rounded all his
life with music. Tennyson was in his eighty-first year,
when there "came in a moment" the crown of his
work, the immortal lyric, *Crossing the Bar.* It is hardly
less majestic and musical in the perfect Greek rendering
by his brother-in-law, Mr Lushington. For once at least
a poem has been "poured from the golden to the silver
cup" without the spilling of a drop. The new book's appearance was coincident with the death of Mr Browning,
"so loving and appreciative," as Lady Tennyson wrote ;
a friend, not a rival, however the partisans of either
poet might strive to stir emulation between two men of
such lofty and such various genius.

X.

1890.

In the year 1889 the poet's health had permitted him to take long walks on the sea-shore and along the cliffs, one of which, by reason of its whiteness, he had named "Taliessin," "the splendid brow." His mind ran on a poem founded on an Egyptian legend (of which the source is not mentioned), telling how "despair and death came upon him who was mad enough to try to probe the secret of the universe." He also thought of a drama on Tristram, who, in the Idylls, is treated with brevity, and not with the sympathy of the old writer who cries, "God bless Tristram the knight: he fought for England!" But early in 1890 Tennyson suffered from a severe attack of influenza. In May Mr Watts painted his portrait, and

"Divinely through all hindrance found the man."

Tennyson was a great admirer of Miss Austen's novels: "The realism and life-likeness of Miss Austen's *Dramatis Personæ* come nearest to those of Shakespeare. Shakespeare, however, is a sun to which Jane Austen, though a bright and true little world, is but an asteroid." He was therefore pleased to find apple-blossoms co-existing with ripe strawberries on June 28, as Miss Austen has been blamed, by minute philosophers, for introducing this combination in the garden party in *Emma*. The poet, like most of the good and great, read novels eagerly, and excited himself over the confirmation of an adult male in a story by Miss Yonge. Of Scott, "the most chivalrous literary figure of the century, and the author with the widest range since Shakespeare," he preferred *Old Mortality*, and it is a good choice. He hated "morbid and introspective tales, with their oceans of sham philosophy." At this time, with catholic taste, he read Mr Stevenson and Mr Meredith, Miss Braddon and Mr Henry James, Ouida and Mr Thomas Hardy; Mr Hall Caine and Mr Anstey; Mrs Oliphant and Miss Edna Lyall. Not everybody can peruse all of these very diverse authors with pleasure. He began his poem on the Roman gladiatorial combats; indeed his years, fourscore and one, left his intellectual eagerness as unimpaired as that of Goethe. "A crooked share," he said to the Princess Louise, "may make a straight furrow." "One afternoon he had a long waltz with M—— in the ballroom." Speaking of

> "All the charm of all the Muses
> Often flowering in a lonely word"

in Virgil, he adduced, rather strangely, the *cunctantem*

ramum, said of the Golden Bough, in the Sixth Æneid. The choice is odd, because the Sibyl has just told Æneas that, if he be destined to pluck the branch of gold, *ipse volens facilisque sequetur*, " it will come off of its own accord," like the sacred *ti* branches of the Fijians, which bend down to be plucked for the Fire rite. Yet, when the predestined Æneas tries to pluck the bough of gold, it yields *reluctantly* (*cunctantem*), contrary to what the Sibyl has foretold. Mr Conington, therefore, thought the phrase a slip on the part of Virgil. " People accused Virgil of plagiarising," he said, " but if a man made it his own there was no harm in that (look at the great poets, Shakespeare included)." Tennyson, like Virgil, made much that was ancient his own ; his verses are often, and purposefully, a mosaic of classical reminiscences. But he was vexed by the hunters after remote and unconscious resemblances, and far - fetched analogies between his lines and those of others. He complained that, if he said that the sun went down, a parallel was at once cited from Homer, or anybody else, and he used a very powerful phrase to condemn critics who detected such repetitions. " The moanings of the homeless sea," —" moanings " from Horace, " homeless " from Shelley. " As if no one else had ever heard the sea moan except Horace ! " Tennyson's mixture of memory and forgetfulness was not so strange as that of Scott, and when he adapted from the Greek, Latin, or Italian, it was of set purpose, just as it was with Virgil. The

beautiful lines comparing a girl's eyes to bottom agates
that seem to

> " Wave and float
> In crystal currents of clear running seas,"

he invented while bathing in Wales.   It was his habit to
note down in verse such similes from nature, and to use
them when he found occasion.   But the higher criticism,
analysing the simile, detected elements from Shakespeare
and from Beaumont and Fletcher.

In June 1891 the poet went on a tour in Devonshire,
and began his *Akbar*, and probably wrote *June Bracken
and Heather ;* or perhaps it was composed when "we
often sat on the top of Blackdown to watch the sunset."
He wrote to Mr Kipling—

> " The oldest to the youngest singer
> That England bore "

(to alter Mr Swinburne's lines to Landor), praising his
Flag of England.   Mr Kipling replied as " the private
to the general."

Early in 1892 *The Foresters* was successfully pro-
duced at New York by Miss Ada Rehan, the music by
Sir Arthur Sullivan, and the scenery from woodland
designs by Whymper.   Robin Hood (as we learn from
Mark Twain) is a favourite hero with the youth of
America.   Mr Tom Sawyer himself took, in Mark
Twain's tale, the part of the bold outlaw.

The Death of Œnone was published in 1892, with the
dedication to the Master of Balliol—

" Read a Grecian tale retold
Which, cast in later Grecian mould,
Quintus Calaber
Somewhat lazily handled of old."

Quintus Calaber, more usually called Quintus Smyrnæus, is a writer of perhaps the fourth century of our era. About him nothing, or next to nothing, is known. He told, in so late an age, the conclusion of the Tale of Troy, and (in the writer's opinion) has been unduly neglected and disdained. His manner, I venture to think, is more Homeric than that of the more famous and doubtless greater Alexandrian poet of the Argonautic cycle, Apollonius Rhodius, his senior by five centuries. His materials were probably the ancient and lost poems of the Epic Cycle, and the story of the death of Œnone may be from the *Little Iliad* of Lesches. Possibly parts of his work may be textually derived from the Cyclics, but the topic is very obscure. In Quintus, Paris, after encountering evil omens on his way, makes a long speech, imploring the pardon of the deserted Œnone. She replies, not with the Tennysonian brevity ; she sends him back to the helpless arms of her rival, Helen. Paris dies on the hills ; never did Helen see him returning. The wood-nymphs bewail Paris, and a herdsman brings the bitter news to Helen, who chants her lament. But remorse falls on Œnone. She does not go

" Slowly down
By the long torrent's ever-deepened roar,"

but rushes "swift as the wind to seek and spring upon the pyre of her lord." Fate and Aphrodite drive her headlong, and in heaven Selene, remembering Endymion, bewails the lot of her sister in sorrow. Œnone reaches the funeral flame, and without a word or a cry leaps into her husband's arms, the wild Nymphs wondering. The lovers are mingled in one heap of ashes, and these are bestowed in one vessel of gold and buried in a howe. This is the story which the poet rehandled in his old age, completing the work of his happy youth when he walked with Hallam in the Pyrenean hills, that were to him as Ida. The romance of Œnone and her death condone, as even Homer was apt to condone, the sins of beautiful Paris, whom the nymphs lament, despite the evil that he has wrought. The silence of the veiled Œnone, as she springs into her lover's last embrace, is perhaps more affecting and more natural than Tennyson's

> " She lifted up a voice
> Of shrill command, ' Who burns upon the pyre ? ' "

The *St Telemachus* has the old splendour and vigour of verse, and, though written so late in life, is worthy of the poet's prime :—

> " Eve after eve that haggard anchorite
> Would haunt the desolated fane, and there
> Gaze at the ruin, often mutter low
> ' Vicisti Galilæe ' ; louder again,
> Spurning a shatter'd fragment of the God,
> ' Vicisti Galilæe ! ' but—when now
> Bathed in that lurid crimson—ask'd ' Is earth

On fire to the West? or is the Demon-god
Wroth at his fall?' and heard an answer 'Wake
Thou deedless dreamer, lazying out a life
Of self-suppression, not of selfless love.'
And once a flight of shadowy fighters crost
The disk, and once, he thought, a shape with wings
Came sweeping by him, and pointed to the West,
And at his ear he heard a whisper ' Rome,'
And in his heart he cried ' The call of God !'
And call'd arose, and, slowly plunging down
Thro' that disastrous glory, set his face
By waste and field and town of alien tongue,
Following a hundred sunsets, and the sphere
Of westward-wheeling stars ; and every dawn
Struck from him his own shadow on to Rome.
    Foot-sore, way-worn, at length he touch'd his goal,
The Christian city."

Akbar's Dream may be taken, more or less, to
represent the poet's own theology of a race seeking after
God, if perchance they may find Him, and the closing
Hymn was a favourite with Tennyson.　He said, " It is
a magnificent metre " :—

" HYMN.

I.

Once again thou flamest heavenward, once again we see
      thee rise.
Every morning is thy birthday gladdening human hearts
      and eyes.
    Every morning here we greet it, bowing lowly down
      before thee,
Thee the Godlike, thee the changeless in thine ever-chang-
      ing skies.

II.

Shadow-maker, shadow-slayer, arrowing light from clime
    to clime,
Hear thy myriad laureates hail thee monarch in their wood-
    land rhyme.
    Warble bird, and open flower, and, men, below the
        dome of azure
Kneel adoring Him the Timeless in the flame that measures
    Time ! "

In this final volume the poet cast his handful of
incense on the altar of Scott, versifying the tale of *Il
Bizarro*, which the dying Sir Walter records in his
Journal in Italy. *The Churchwarden and the Curate*
is not inferior to the earlier peasant poems in its expression of shrewdness, humour, and superstition. A verse
of *Poets and Critics* may be taken as the poet's last word
on the old futile quarrel :—

    " This thing, that thing is the rage,
    Helter-skelter runs the age ;
    Minds on this round earth of ours
    Vary like the leaves and flowers,
      Fashion'd after certain laws ;
    Sing thou low or loud or sweet,
    All at all points thou canst not meet,
      Some will pass and some will pause.

    What is true at last will tell :
    Few at first will place thee well ;
    Some too low would have thee shine,
    Some too high—no fault of thine—
      Hold thine own, and work thy will !
    Year will graze the heel of year,
    But seldom comes the poet here,
      And the Critic's rarer still."

Still the lines hold good—

> " Some too low would have thee shine,
> Some too high—no fault of thine."

The end was now at hand.   A sense of weakness was
felt by the poet on September 3, 1892 : on the 28th
his family sent for Sir Andrew Clark ; but the patient
gradually faded out of life, and expired on Thursday,
October 6, at 1.35 A.M.   To the very last he had
Shakespeare by him, and his windows were open to the
sun ; on the last night they were flooded by the moon-
light.   The description of the final scenes must be read
in the Biography by the poet's son.   " His patience and
quiet strength had power upon those who were nearest
and dearest to him ; we felt thankful for the love and
the utter peace of it all."   " The life after death,"
Tennyson had said just before his fatal illness, " is the
cardinal point of Christianity.   I believe that God
reveals Himself in every individual soul ; and my idea
of Heaven is the perpetual ministry of one soul to
another."   He had lived the life of heaven upon earth,
being in all his work a minister of things honourable,
lovely, consoling, and ennobling to the souls of others,
with a ministry which cannot die.   His body sleeps next
to that of his friend and fellow-poet, Robert Browning,
in front of Chaucer's monument in the Abbey.

XI. LAST CHAPTER.

" O, THAT Press will get hold of me now," Tennyson said when he knew that his last hour was at hand. He had a horror of personal tattle, as even his early poems declare—

> " For now the Poet cannot die,
>   Nor leave his music as of old,
>   But round him ere he scarce be cold
> Begins the scandal and the cry."

But no " carrion-vulture " has waited

> " To tear his heart before the crowd."

About Tennyson, doubtless, there is much anecdotage : most of the anecdotes turn on his shyness, his really exaggerated hatred of personal notoriety, and the odd and brusque things which he would say when alarmed by effusive strangers. It has not seemed worth while to repeat more than one or two of these legends, nor have I sought outside the Biography by his son for more than the biographer chose to tell. The readers who are least interested in poetry are most interested in tattle about the poet. It is the privilege of genius to retain

the freshness and simplicity, with some of the foibles, of
the child. When Tennyson read his poems aloud he
was apt to be moved by them, and to express frankly
his approbation where he thought it deserved. Only
very rudimentary psychologists recognised conceit in
this freedom ; and only the same set of persons mistook
shyness for arrogance. Effusiveness of praise or curiosity
in a stranger is apt to produce bluntness of reply in a
Briton. "Don't talk d——d nonsense, sir," said the
Duke of Wellington to the gushing person who piloted
him, in his old age, across Piccadilly. Of Tennyson
Mr Palgrave says, "I have known him silenced, almost
frozen, before the eager unintentional eyes of a girl of
fifteen. And under the stress of this nervous impulse compelled to contradict his inner self (especially
when under the terror of leonisation . . .), he was
doubtless at times betrayed into an abrupt phrase,
a cold unsympathetic exterior ; a moment's 'defect
of the rose.'" Had he not been sensitive in all
things, he would have been less of a poet. The chief
criticism directed against his mode of life is that he *was*
sensitive and reserved, but he could and did make
himself pleasant in the society of *les pauvres d'esprit.*
Curiosity alarmed him, and drove him into his shell :
strangers who met him in that mood carried away false
impressions, which developed into myths. As the
Master of Balliol has recorded, despite his shyness "he
was extremely hospitable, often inviting not only his
friends, but the friends of his friends, and giving them a

hearty welcome. For underneath a sensitive exterior he was thoroughly genial if he was understood." In these points he was unlike his great contemporary, Browning; for instance, Tennyson never (I think) was the Master's guest at Balliol, mingling, like Browning, with the undergraduates, to whom the Master's hospitality was freely extended. Yet, where he was familiar, Tennyson was a gay companion, not shunning jest or even paradox. "As Dr Johnson says, every man may be judged of by his laughter": but no Boswell has chronicled the laughters of Tennyson. "He never, or hardly ever, made puns or witticisms" (though one pun, at least, endures in tradition), "but always lived in an attitude of humour." Mr Jowett writes (and no description of the poet is better than his)—

If I were to describe his outward appearance, I should say that he was certainly unlike any one else whom I ever saw. A glance at some of Watts' portraits of him will give, better than any description which can be expressed in words, a conception of his noble mien and look. He was a magnificent man, who stood before you in his native refinement and strength. The unconventionality of his manners was in keeping with the originality of his figure. He would sometimes say nothing, or a word or two only, to the stranger who approached him, out of shyness. He would sometimes come into the drawing-room reading a book. At other times, especially to ladies, he was singularly gracious and benevolent. He would talk about the accidents of his own life with an extraordinary freedom, as at the moment they appeared to present themselves to his mind, the days of his boyhood that were passed at Somersby, and the old school of manners which he came across in his own neighbour-

hood : the days of the "apostles" at Cambridge : the years
which he spent in London ; the evenings enjoyed at the
Cock Tavern, and elsewhere, when he saw another side
of life, not without a kindly and humorous sense of the
ridiculous in his fellow-creatures.   His repertory of stories
was perfectly inexhaustible ; they were often about slight
matters that would scarcely bear repetition, but were told
with such lifelike reality, that they convulsed his hearers
with laughter.   Like most story-tellers, he often repeated
his favourites ; but, like children, his audience liked hearing
them again and again, and he enjoyed telling them.   It
might be said of him that he told more stories than any one,
but was by no means the regular story-teller.   In the com-
monest conversation he showed himself a man of genius.

  To this description may be added another by Mr F.
T. Palgrave :—

  Every one will have seen men, distinguished in some line
of work, whose conversation (to take the old figure) either
"smelt too strongly of the lamp," or lay quite apart from
their art or craft.   What, through all these years, struck me
about Tennyson, was that whilst he never deviated into
poetical language as such, whether in rhetoric or highly
coloured phrase, yet throughout the substance of his talk
the same mode of thought, the same imaginative grasp of
nature, the same fineness and gentleness in his view of
character, the same forbearance and toleration, the *aurea
mediocritas* despised by fools and fanatics, which are stamped
on his poetry, were constantly perceptible : whilst in the easy
and as it were unsought choiceness, the conscientious and
truth - loving precision of his words, the same personal
identity revealed itself.   What a strange charm lay here ;
how deeply illuminating the whole character, as in prolonged
intercourse it gradually revealed itself !   Artist and man,
Tennyson was invariably true to himself, or rather, in
Wordsworth's phrase, he "moved altogether" ; his nature

and his poetry being harmonious aspects of the same soul; as botanists tell us that flower and fruit are but transformations of root and stem and leafage. We read how, in mediæval days, conduits were made to flow with claret. But this was on great occasions only. Tennyson's fountain always ran wine.

Once more: In Mme. Récamier's *salon*, I have read, at the time when conversation was yet a fine art in Paris, guests famous for *esprit* would sit in the twilight round the stove, whilst each in turn let fly some sparkling anecdote or bon-mot, which rose and shone and died out into silence, till the next of the elect pyrotechnists was ready. Good things of this kind, as I have said, were plentiful in Tennyson's repertory. But what, to pass from the materials to the method of his conversation, eminently marked it was the continuity of the electric current. He spoke, and was silent, and spoke again: but the circuit was unbroken; there was no effort in taking up the thread, no sense of disjunction. Often I thought, had he never written a line of the poems so dear to us, his conversation alone would have made him the most interesting companion known to me. From this great and gracious student of humanity, what less, indeed, could be expected? And if, as a converser, I were to compare him with Socrates, as figured for us in the dialogues of his great disciple, I think that I should have the assent of that eminently valued friend of Tennyson's, whose long labour of love has conferred English citizenship upon Plato.

We have called him shy and sensitive in daily intercourse with strangers, and as to criticism, he freely confessed that a midge of dispraise could sting, while applause gave him little pleasure. Yet no poet altered his verses so much in obedience to censure unjustly or irritatingly stated, yet in essence just. He readily rejected some of his "Juvenilia" on Mr Palgrave's suggestion. The same friend tells how well he took a rather fierce attack on an unpublished piece, when Mr Palgrave "owned that he could not find one good line in it." Very few poets, or even versifiers (fiercer they than poets are), would have continued to show their virgin numbers to a friend so candid, as Tennyson did. Perhaps most of the *genus irritabile* will grant that spoken criticism, if unfavourable, somehow annoys and stirs opposition in an author; probably because it confirms his own suspicions about his work. Such criticism is almost invariably just. But Campbell, when Rogers offered a correction, "bounced out of the room, with a 'Hang it! I should like to see the man who would dare to correct me.'"

Mr Jowett justly recognised in the life of Tennyson two circumstances which made him other than, but for these, he would have been. He had intended to do with the Arthurian subject what he never did, "in some way or other to have represented in it the great religions of the world. . . . It is a proof of Tennyson's genius that he should have thus early grasped the great historical aspect of religion." His intention was foiled, his early dream was broken, by the death of Arthur Hallam, and by the coldness and contempt with which, at the same period, his early poems were received.

Mr Jowett (who had a firm belief in the "great work") regretted the change of plan as to the Arthurian topic, regretted it the more from his own interest in the

History of Religion. But we need not share the regrets. The early plan for the Arthur (which Mr Jowett never saw) has been published, and certainly the scheme could not have been executed on these lines.[1] Moreover, as the Master observed, the work would have been premature in Tennyson's youth, and, indeed, it would still be premature. The comparative science of religious evolution is even now very tentative, and does not yield materials of sufficient stability for an epic, even if such an epic could be forced into the mould of the Arthur legends, a feat perhaps impossible, and certainly undesirable. A truly fantastic allegory must have been the result, and it is fortunate that the poet abandoned the idea in favour of more human themes. Moreover, he recognised very early that his was not a Muse *de longue haleine ;* that he must be " short." We may therefore feel certain that his early sorrow and discouragement were salutary to him as a poet, and as a man. He became more sympathetic, more tender, and was obliged to put forth that stoical self-control, and strenuous courage and endurance, through which alone his poetic career was rendered possible. " He had the susceptibility of a child or a woman," says his friend ; " he had also " (it was a strange combination) " the strength of a giant or of a god." Without these qualities he must have broken down between 1833 and 1842 into a hypochondriac, or a morose, if majestic, failure. Poor, obscure, and unhappy, he overcame the world, and passed from darkness

[1] See the *Life,* 1899, p. 521.

into light. The "poetic temperament" in another not gifted with his endurance and persistent strength would have achieved ruin.

Most of us remember Taine's parallel between Tennyson and Alfred de Musset. The French critic has no high approval of Tennyson's "respectability" and long peaceful life, as compared with the wrecked life and genius of Musset, *l'enfant perdu* of love, wine, and song. This is a theory like another, and is perhaps attractive to the young. The poet must have strong passions, or how can he sing of them : he must be tossed and whirled in the stress of things, like Shelley's autumn leaves,—

"Ghosts from an enchanter fleeing."

Looking at Burns, Byron, Musset, or even at Shelley's earlier years, youth sees in them the true poets, "sacred things," but also "light," as Plato says, inspired to break their wings against the nature of existence, and the *flammantia mœnia mundi*. But this is almost a boyish idea, this idea that the true poet is the slave of the passions, and that the poet who dominates them has none, and is but a staid domestic animal, an ass browsing the common, as somebody has written about Wordsworth. Certainly Tennyson's was no "passionless perfection." He, like others, was tempted to beat with ineffectual wings against the inscrutable nature of life. He, too, had his dark hour, and was as subject to temptation as they who yielded to the stress and died,

or became unhappy waifs, "young men with a splendid
past." He must have known, no less than Musset, the
attractions of many a *paradis artificiel*, with its bright
visions, its houris, its offers of oblivion of pain. "He
had the look of one who had suffered greatly," Mr
Palgrave writes in his record of their first meeting in
1842. But he, like Goethe, Scott, and Victor Hugo,
had strength as well as passion and emotion; he came
unscorched through the fire that has burned away the
wings of so many other great poets. This was no less
fortunate for the world than for himself. Of his prolonged dark hour we know little in detail, but we have
seen that from the first he resisted the Tempter; *Ulysses*
is his *Retro Sathanas !*

About "the mechanism of genius" in Tennyson Mr
Palgrave has told us a little; more appears incidentally
in his biography. "It was his way that when we had
entered on some scene of special beauty or grandeur,
after enjoying it together, he should always withdraw
wholly from sight, and study the view, as it were, in a
little artificial solitude."

Tennyson's poems, Mr Palgrave says, often arose in
a kind of *point de repère* (like those forms and landscapes which seem to spring from a floating point of
light, beheld with closed eyes just before we sleep).
"More than once he said that his poems sprang often
from a 'nucleus,' some one word, maybe, or brief
melodious phrase, which had floated through the brain,
as it were, unbidden. And perhaps at once while walk-

ing they were presently wrought into a little song. But if he did not write it down at once the lyric fled from him irrecoverably." He believed himself thus to have lost poems as good as his best. It seems probable that this is a common genesis of verses, good or bad, among all who write. Like Dickens, and like most men of genius probably, he saw all the scenes of his poems "in his mind's eye." Many authors do this, without the power of making their readers share the vision; but probably few can impart the vision who do not themselves "visualise" with distinctness. We have seen, in the cases of *The Holy Grail* and other pieces, that Tennyson, after long meditating a subject, often wrote very rapidly, and with little need of correction. He was born with "style"; it was a gift of his genius rather than the result of conscious elaboration. Yet he did use "the file," of which much is now written, especially for the purpose of polishing away the sibilants, so common in our language. In the nine years of silence which followed the little book of 1833 his poems matured, and henceforth it is probable that he altered his verses little, if we except the modifications in *The Princess*. Many slight verbal touches were made, or old readings were restored, but important changes, in the way of omission or addition, became rare.

Of nature Tennyson was scrupulously observant till his very latest days, eagerly noting, not only "effects," as a painter does, but their causes, botanical or

geological. Had man been scientific from the beginning he would probably have evolved no poetry at all;
material things would not have been endowed by him
with life and passion; he would have told himself no
stories of the origins of stars and flowers, clouds and fire,
winds and rainbows. Modern poets have resented, like
Keats and Wordsworth, the destruction of the old prehistoric dreams by the geologist and by other scientific
characters. But it was part of Tennyson's poetic
originality to see the beautiful things of nature at once
with the vision of early poetic men, and of moderns
accustomed to the microscope, telescope, spectrum
analysis, and so forth. Thus Tennyson received a
double delight from the sensible universe, and it is a
double delight that he communicates to his readers.
His intellect was thus always active, even in apparent
repose. His eyes rested not from observing, or his
mind from recording and comparing, the beautiful
familiar phenomena of earth and sky. In the matter
of the study of books we have seen how deeply
versed he was in certain of the Greek, Roman, and
Italian classics. Mr Jowett writes: "He was what
might be called a good scholar in the university or
public-school sense of the term, . . . yet I seem to
remember that he had his favourite classics, such as
Homer, and Pindar, and Theocritus. . . . He was
also a lover of Greek fragments. But I am not sure
whether, in later life, he ever sat down to read con-
secutively the greatest works of Æschylus and Sophocles,

although he used occasionally to dip into them." The Greek dramatists, in fact, seem to have affected Tennyson's work but slightly, while he constantly reminds us of Virgil, Homer, Theocritus, and even Persius and Horace. Mediæval French, whether in poetry or prose, and the poetry of the "Pleiad" seems to have occupied little of his attention. Into the oriental literatures he dipped — pretty deeply for his *Akbar;* and even his *Locksley Hall* owed something to Sir William Jones's version of "the old Arabian *Moallakat.*" The debt appears to be infinitesimal. He seems to have been less closely familiar with Elizabethan poetry than might have been expected : a number of his *obiter dicta* on all kinds of literary points are recorded in the *Life* by Mr Palgrave. "Sir Walter Scott's short tale, *My Aunt Margaret's Mirror* (how little known !), he once spoke of as the finest of all ghost or magical stories." Lord Tennyson adds, " *The Tapestried Chamber* also he greatly admired." Both are lost from modern view among the short pieces of the last volumes of the *Waverley* novels. Of the poet's interest in and attitude towards the more obscure pyschological and psychical problems—to popular science foolishness—enough has been said, but the remarks of Professor Tyndall have not been cited :—

My special purpose in introducing this poem, however, was to call your attention to a passage further on which greatly interested me. The poem is, throughout, a discussion between a believer in immortality and one who is unable to believe. The method pursued is this.   The Sage reads a portion of the scroll, which he has taken from the hands of his follower, and then brings his own arguments to bear upon that portion, with a view to neutralising the scepticism of the younger man.   Let me here remark that I read the whole series of poems published under the title " Tiresias," full of admiration for their freshness and vigour. Seven years after I had first read them your father died, and you, his son, asked me to contribute a chapter to the book which you contemplate publishing.   I knew that I had some small store of references to my interview with your father carefully written in ancient journals.   On the receipt of your request, I looked up the account of my first visit to Farring-ford, and there, to my profound astonishment, I found described that experience of your father's which, in the mouth of the Ancient Sage, was made the ground of an important argument against materialism and in favour of personal immortality eight-and-twenty years afterwards.   In no other poem during all these years is, to my knowledge, this experience once alluded to.   I had completely forgotten it, but here it was recorded in black and white.   If you turn to your father's account of the wonderful state of consciousness superinduced by thinking of his own name, and compare it with the argument of the Ancient Sage, you will see that they refer to one and the same phenomenon.

> And more, my son ! for more than once when I
> Sat all alone, revolving in myself
> The word that is the symbol of myself,
> The mortal limit of the Self was loosed,
> And past into the Nameless, as a cloud
> Melts into heaven.   I touch'd my limbs, the limbs
> Were strange, not mine—and yet no shade of doubt,
> But utter clearness, and thro' loss of Self
> The gain of such large life as match'd with ours
> Were Sun to spark—unshadowable in words,
> Themselves but shadows of a shadow-world.

Any words about Tennyson as a politician are apt to

excite the sleepless prejudice which haunts the political
field.   He probably, if forced to "put a name to it,"
would have called himself a Liberal.   But he was not a
social agitator.   He never set a rick on fire.   "He held
aloof, in a somewhat detached position, from the great
social seethings of his age" (Mr Frederic Harrison).
But in youth he helped to extinguish some flaming
ricks.   He spoke of the "many-headed beast" (the
reading public) in terms borrowed from Plato.   He
had no higher esteem for mobs than Shakespeare or
John Knox professed, while his theory of tyrants (in the
case of Napoleon III. about 1852) was that of Liberals
like Mr Swinburne and Victor Hugo.   Though to
modern enlightenment Tennyson may seem as great a
Tory as Dr Johnson, yet he had spoken his word in
1852 for the freedom of France, and for securing
England against the supposed designs of a usurper
(now fallen).   He really believed, obsolete as the faith
may be, in guarding our own, both on land and sea.
Perhaps no Continental or American critic has ever
yet dispraised a poetical fellow-countryman merely for
urging the duties of national union and national defence.   A critic, however, writes thus of Tennyson : "When our poet descends into the arena of party
polemics, in such things as *Riflemen, Form !   Hands
all Round*, . . . *The Fleet*, and other topical pieces
dear to the Jingo soul, it is not poetry but journalism."
I doubt whether the desirableness of the existence of a
volunteer force and of a fleet really is within the arena of

P

party polemics. If any party thinks that we ought to have no volunteers, and that it is our duty to starve the fleet, what is that party's name? Who cries, "Down with the Fleet! Down with National Defence! Hooray for the Disintegration of the Empire!"?

Tennyson was not a party man, but he certainly would have opposed any such party. If to defend our homes and this England be "Jingoism," Tennyson, like Shakespeare, was a Jingo. But, alas! I do not know the name of the party which opposes Tennyson, and which wishes the invader to trample down England—any invader will do for so philanthropic a purpose. Except when resisting this unnamed party, the poet seldom or never entered "the arena of party polemics." Tennyson could not have exclaimed, like Squire Western, "Hurrah for old England! Twenty thousand honest Frenchmen have landed in Kent!" He undeniably did write verses (whether poetry or journalism) tending to make readers take an unfavourable view of honest invaders. If to do that is to be a "Jingo," and if such conduct hurts the feelings of any great English party, then Tennyson was a Jingo and a partisan, and was, so far, a rhymester, like Mr Kipling. Indeed we know that Tennyson applauded Mr Kipling's *The English Flag.* So the worst is out, as we in England count the worst. In America and on the continent of Europe, however, a poet may be proud of his country's flag without incurring rebuke from his countrymen. Tennyson did not reckon himself a party man; he believed more in political evolution than in political revolution, with cataclysms. He was neither an Anarchist nor a Home Ruler, nor a politician so generous as to wish England to be laid defenceless at the feet of her foes.

If these sentiments deserve censure, in Tennyson, at least, they claim our tolerance. He was not born in a generation late enough to be truly Liberal. Old prejudices about "this England," old words from *Henry V.* and *King John*, haunted his memory and darkened his vision of the true proportions of things. We draw in prejudice with our mother's milk. The mother of Tennyson had not been an Agnostic or a Comtist; his father had not been a staunch true-blue anti-Englander. Thus he inherited a certain bias in favour of faith and fatherland, a bias from which he could never emancipate himself. But *tout comprendre c'est tout pardonner.* Had Tennyson's birth been later, we might find in him a more complete realisation of our poetic ideal—might have detected less to blame or to forgive.

With that apology we must leave the fame of Tennyson as a politician to the clement consideration of an enlightened posterity. I do not defend his narrow insularities, his Jingoism, or the appreciable percentage of faith which blushing analysis may detect in his honest doubt : these things I may regret or condemn, but we ought not to let them obscure our view of the Poet. He was led away by bad examples. Of all Jingoes

Shakespeare is the most unashamed, and next to him
are Drayton, Scott, and Wordsworth, with his

" Oh, for one hour of that Dundee ! "

In the years which followed the untoward affair of
Waterloo young Tennyson fell much under the influence
of Shakespeare, Wordsworth, and the other offenders,
and these are extenuating circumstances.   By a curious
practical paradox, where the realms of poetry and politics
meet, the Tory critics seem milder of mood and more
Liberal than the Liberal critics.   Thus Mr William
Morris was certainly a very advanced political theorist ;
and in theology Mr Swinburne has written things not
easily reconcilable with orthodoxy.   Yet we find Divine-
Right Tories, who in literature are fervent admirers of
these two poets, and leave their heterodoxies out of
account.   But many Liberal critics appear unable quite
to forgive Tennyson because he did not wish to starve
the fleet, and because he held certain very ancient, if
obsolete, beliefs.   Perhaps a general amnesty ought to
be passed, as far as poets are concerned, and their
politics and creeds should be left to silence, where
" beyond these voices there is peace."

One remark, I hope, can excite no prejudice.   The
greatest of the Gordons was a soldier, and lived in
religion.   But the point at which Tennyson's memory is
blended with that of Gordon is the point of sympathy
with the neglected poor.   It is to his wise advice, and to
affection for Gordon, that we owe the Gordon training

school for poor boys,—a good school, and good boys
come out of that academy.

The question as to Tennyson's precise rank in the
glorious roll of the Poets of England can never be
determined by us, if in any case or at any time such
determinations can be made.   We do not, or should not,
ask whether Virgil or Lucretius, whether Æschylus or
Sophocles, is the greater poet.   The consent of mankind
seems to place Homer and Shakespeare and Dante high
above all.   For the rest no prize-list can be settled.   If
influence among aliens is the test, Byron probably takes,
among our poets, the next rank after Shakespeare.   But
probably there is no possible test.   In certain respects
Shelley, in many respects Milton, in some Coleridge, in
some Burns, in the opinion of a number of persons
Browning, are greater poets than Tennyson.   But for
exquisite variety and varied exquisiteness Tennyson is
not readily to be surpassed.   At one moment he pleases
the uncritical mass of readers, in another mood he wins
the verdict of the *raffiné*.   It is a success which scarce
any English poet but Shakespeare has excelled.   His
faults have rarely, if ever, been those of flat - footed,
"thick-ankled" dulness ; of rhetoric, of common-place ;
rather have his defects been the excess of his qualities.
A kind of John Bullishness may also be noted, especially
in derogatory references to France, which, true or untrue,
are out of taste and keeping.   But these errors could be
removed by the excision of half-a-dozen lines.   His later
work (as the *Voyage of Maeldune*) shows a just apprecia-

tion of ancient Celtic literature.　A great critic, F. T.
Palgrave, has expressed perhaps the soundest appreciation of Tennyson :—

It is for "the days that remain" to bear witness to
his real place in the great hierarchy, amongst whom Dante
boldly yet justly ranked himself.　But if we look at
Tennyson's work in a twofold aspect, — *Here*, on the
exquisite art in which, throughout, his verse is clothed, the
lucid beauty of the form, the melody almost audible as music,
the mysterious skill by which the words used constantly
strike as the *inevitable* words (and hence, unforgettable), the
subtle allusive touches, by which a secondary image is suggested to enrich the leading thought, as the harmonic
"partials" give richness to the note struck upon the string ;
There, when we think of the vast fertility in subject and
treatment, united with happy selection of motive, the wide
range of character, the dramatic force of impersonation, the
pathos in every variety, the mastery over the comic and the
tragic alike, above all, perhaps, those phrases of luminous
insight which spring direct from imaginative observation of
Humanity, true for all time, coming from the heart to the
heart,—his work will probably be found to lie somewhere
between that of Virgil and Shakespeare : having its portion,
if I may venture on the phrase, in the inspiration of both.

A professed enthusiast for Tennyson can add nothing
to, and take nothing from, these words of one who,
though his friend, was too truly a critic to entertain
the admiration that goes beyond idolatry.

INDEX.

THE END.